Christopher Lowell's
Seven Layers of Design

Christopher Lowell's Seven Layers

3 4 5 6 7

# of Design

Fearless, Fabulous Decorating

Clarkson Potter/Publishers
New York

Photographs by Douglas Hill
Additional photography by Gary Kellner (p. 6 bottom), Greg Parks
(p. 6 top), Lee Salem (p. 170), and Pamela Young (pp. 13, 14 right,
20, 21, 24, 26)
Illustrations by Rik Olson

Originally published in hardcover in slightly different form by
Discovery Books, an imprint of Random House, Inc., New York, in
2000.

Library of Congress Cataloging-in-Publication Data is available upon
request.

ISBN 1-4000-8270-6

Printed in the United States of America

10 9 8 7 6 5 4 3 2 1

First Paperback Edition

Contents

Foreword

Before

During

It's 1992, and a bleak winter day in Chagrin Falls, Ohio. I'm flipping through the channels. Norm is working on a drop-leaf table using tools I've never seen before. Bob is demonstrating how to use a jackhammer to remove a concrete floor. And Martha is painstakingly gold-leafing persimmon branches picked from her own yard. None of them is smiling.

Meanwhile, I'm living illegally in my studio/office. Wintry weather has eclipsed any hope of turning Christopher Lowell's retail shop into the empire I had dreamed of. How could I know that this picturesque little town, in summer the biggest tourist attraction outside Cleveland, was in winter a retail hell frozen over?

After three years of local TV appearances, camping on editors' doorsteps, and hauling my trunk show to every woman's club in town, I was no further ahead than the day I arrived, raffia in hand, to take this small community by storm. With every month that passed, the home-improvement market continued to explode and yet another how-to show hit the airwaves. Where had I gone wrong? I'd been in the theater, performed as a concert pianist, had success both as a fine artist and a corporate art director. In fact it was this eclectic background that had inspired my home-decorating dream in the first place. But now it was all doom and gloom.

What sometimes comes in the moment of greatest despair is that calm, still voice. Mine came to me as a haunting, eight-word phrase from the past: "Where there is fear, there is no creativity." Many years before, while attending college back East, I had created a class called "Creativity 101" based on my own curiosity about the creative process. Why was it that some people were so damn creative and others seemed to possess little sign of it? How come some people have extraordinary bursts of genius, but then for some reason lost it?

What I had learned so vividly was that *fear* was the greatest inhibitor of creativity. By giving up the ego, the pressure to be perfect, and the judgment of others, we return to a childlike state where we feel safe to make mistakes. I had forgotten this lesson. In my striving for success I had lost that childlike quality. I smiled; that's what had been missing from all those how-to shows. It wasn't about home improvement, it was about self-esteem.

And what a great arena to explore personal creativity—the HOME. After all it's the most personal reflection of who we are. It's our little universe! I made the decision, that very night, to get rid of the retail shop and turn the entire space into an educational center. My staff and I printed up flyers that offered a variety of classes ranging from marbleizing to topiary, and a class we called Decorating 911. I, in my infinite wisdom, would answer questions and dispense advice. Each person would get a half-hour devoted to their needs, and exchange ideas with each other.

These fabulous women who had caught our dream early were a real cross-section. Among them were young wives who found themselves relocated far from city life, single women, new brides, soccer moms, empty nesters, and retired women. These ladies shared their candor and dedication freely with us. Together our biggest challenge was to create a template that would work regardless of floor plan, budget, and individual taste. It soon became clear that we had to break down the process of decorating a room into specific, sequential steps. We began with 149 layers. Over time, we whittled them down to seven.

What became clear early on was that the content took a back seat to psychology. I was amazed at how these women made choices more with their instincts than with the information we provided. But what I found most fascinating was how their choices had a direct relationship to their self-esteem.

One woman's fear of sewing came from a high-school nightmare. She had been forced to model a monstrosity of an outfit she had made at home, embarrassing herself in front of her peers. Another woman, having felt dominated by her mother, could not make a choice to save her life. The concept of a personal style seemed terrifying to her.

I was also amazed at the amount of myth and misinformation about home design. For instance, many had heard that you find a patterned fabric, then build an entire room around it. In fact the money you'd spend on paint, sofas, and expensive accessories could add up to thousands of dollars. Did it make sense to stack those kinds of investments against ten yards of accent fabric? It was this kind of common sense that helped shape my Seven Layers of Design.

Over the next three years some 3,000 students graduated from our classes, having implemented the Seven Layers in their own homes. We also shot more than 2,000 hours of documentary footage. Little did we know that this footage would inspire what would one day be the most successful daytime program on the Discovery Channel.

After

We've distilled all of our practical techniques and hard-won knowledge into this book. It's laid out in a sequential fashion so that you can benefit from a process that we know works. In addition to dispensing advice, tips, and shortcuts, the text is designed to make you smile and remind you that it's just stuff, not brain surgery.

And remember that fear is the number-one reason why things remain the same in the home. By dispelling fear, you unleash your creativity. Yes, I hope you pick the right sofa and yes, I hope you can make feathering your nest an enjoyable experience. But more important I hope you understand that your environment should be a reflection of who you are. This has less to do with money and more to do with your spiritual well-being. We are how we live.

Christopher Lowell

The Seven Layers of Design

IF YOU CAN PUT AN OUTFIT TOGETHER, you're already overqualified to design a room. And I can prove it. We did an experiment on my show where we turned three women loose in a clothing boutique. In less than an hour each woman had assembled three complete outfits and had a ball doing it. We took the same women to a home superstore and after three hours of torture they left the store empty-handed.

Why was it that, in a clothing boutique they could make effective choices, yet in a home store they freaked out? Putting an outfit together involves color, pattern, texture, accessories, proportion, and comfort. Designing a room is exactly the same. What was the difference? Courage and confidence! Every woman has an instinct for what looks good on her. She understands the concept of enhancement as well as the art of disguise. If she makes a mistake, the outfit can be returned or relegated to the back of the closet. But thirty yards of the wrong wallpaper, permanently installed and on display for the world to critique—that's a different story. Divorces have happened over lesser failings.

The fact is, when I started doing interior design I broke into a sweat every time a client viewed the results of my handiwork. Spending other people's money was nerve-racking, not to mention the refereeing between skeptical husbands and vacillating wives. But, hundreds of rooms later, I got good at it and even picked up some tricks along the way. So now you can benefit from my mistakes.

The most important thing I've learned is that organization is key. Teaching this concept to beginners forced me to condense and simplify the steps, and make sure that even the faintest of heart could do the job without being overwhelmed. Thus after years of trial and error the original 149 layers were distilled into my Seven Layers of Design.

As you read this first section you'll understand that a room is not built all at once but instead layered in seven distinct steps. Think of it as a big board game. You have to follow the path until you're "home."

And as you start to understand how to create your room one layer at a time, my hope is that you'll begin to allow your personal creativity to come out and play. And I promise that, once you see tangible proof of your own imagination, you'll be hooked. So take a deep breath, throw away everything you've heard about interior design and let's begin. You can do it!

Layer One: **Paint & Architecture**

Layer Two: **Installed Flooring**

Layer Three: **Upholstered Furniture**

Layer Four: **Accent Fabrics**

Layer Five: **Non-upholstered Furniture**

Layer Six: **Accessories**

Layer Seven: **Plants & Lighting**

9

1 Paint & Architecture

This hallway and dining room may look empty, but they're actually full of Layer One detail: crown molding, corbels, door and window molding, arches, and a dramatic window.

This first of the Seven Layers is devoted to what I call the "shell" of the room. Don't even think about the other layers to come. That shell consists of five walls. Why five? Look up, my dear. That thing over your head is perhaps the most neg-lected surface in your home. The ceiling is a major expanse that, left bare, can ruin the room's intended design. By understanding that this hard-to-furnish surface is critical for achieving a designer look, you will see why ignoring the ceiling prevents you from establishing a complete environment. But first let's deal with the environment you already have.

You would be amazed how few people have really looked at their living spaces. We tend not to be able to look past our stuff to see the bones of a room. If you are ready to start a makeover, pack all that stuff into boxes, cluster your furniture in the center of the room, and throw a tarp over it. Bye-bye furniture—we'll see you when the paint is dry.

With the distraction of furniture gone, now look at the shape of your room with a fresh eye. What do you love most about the room? Which areas would you like to play up, and which would you like to disguise? The goal is to find—or create—as much character in the room as you can without relying on furniture to do all the work.

The architecture of a room is represented first by its shape and second by its embellishments. A room is highlighted by its wood trim, painted or natural. Baseboards, crown molding, built-ins, fireplace mantels, and window and door trim all add finishing touches to the shell of a room. Later, in the makeover chapters, you'll see where we've added decorative architecture to boxy, charmless rooms to give them substance and interest. Whether a cornice in a window treatment, molding applied to a hollow-core door, a cabinet front, or crown molding, these simple architectural touches can make the difference in giving a room that designer look.

ON THE SURFACE

Countertops are fixed items in a room, and so are considered part of the shell. I've had people tell me that they haven't updated their kitchens because they can't afford to replace the ugly laminate countertops. That's no longer a valid excuse. They can be affordably faux-finished, if only as an interim step. But I have refinished many countertops that have held up brilliantly over the years.

Faux finishing is fairly easy, too. It's important to apply the right primer first as an undercoat. An undercoat primer formulated especially for non-porous surfaces will help the top coat of paint adhere to the surface. Try a

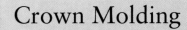

Crown Molding

Dollar for dollar, every inch of molding you add to your room goes right to the bottom line when you sell your home.

And in answer to hundreds of letters, no, I have never met a room, no matter what style, that couldn't benefit from a little crown molding here and there. It needn't be expensive—try trimming two parallel walls in a room with crown molding. It will create the illusion that the entire room is trimmed out. Choose the most visible walls that will help sell the effect and go for it!

Yes, it's a mess, but you can see how color has already transformed this room from stark to stylish. The cream and terra-cotta colors we chose are warm and well suited to this light-filled California home.

These plum-colored bathroom tiles date from the 1920s. To tone them down, we chose a deeper color that created a more balanced, contemporary look, and saved a bundle on retiling.

OPPOSITE: Everything in a room seems darker and heavier with white walls. Imagine the same three pieces —sofa, area rug, and table—surrounded by color.

marbleizing technique, but keep it simple and subtle. You can jazz up counters later with great accessories. Once your faux finish is heavily coated with polyurethane, I guarantee that what was formerly an eyesore will now look fabulous. Sorry, all you procrastinators.

FREEDOM'S WALLS

If you have inherited the oh-so-lovely knotty-pine paneling or the oh-so-cheap veneer paneling, don't despair. This paneling can be disguised to add architectural interest to the room. Knotty pine is quite wonderful if you want a country look, especially if painted. In the Colonial period, rooms were kept small for heating purposes, and most of the interior detail was done in inexpensive pine. To give the paneling an elegant lighter look, it was almost always painted.

I inherited walls of the cheapest veneer paneling in my former shop. With budget a concern, I washed the paneling with soap and water, primed

it, and then painted the paneling the same color as the rest of the trim in the room. To add an architectural embellishment, I capped off the top of each wall with six-inch crown molding. To disguise the fake seams in between the fake panels, I added a thin piece of flat molding over each seam, giving dimension to the wall. At the floor I added a six-inch baseboard. The crown molding and baseboards were also painted the same color as the trim. This treatment transformed an outdated, 1950s office into a charming country cottage.

TILE STYLE

Tile is also fixed and considered part of the shell of the room. Many people inherit strange bathroom colors that are built into the tile work and costly to replace. By surrounding these tiles with the right paint, you can minimize the tile color and make it look intentional. Surrounding bright aqua color with a deep taupe will balance the intensity of the blue. Similarly, salmon

pink tiles can seem to change color when surrounded by a golden mustard color. Start with paint and add finishing touches with matching towels. Before you grab the jackhammer, pick up the paintbrush.

FEAR OF COLOR

This is a good point to talk about the number one fear in home design: choosing color. I receive at least a hundred letters a week from folks asking, pleading, and flipping out about the subject. The thought of having to choose color can make the most courageous break out in a cold sweat. I often hear the same story: "I go to the paint store, stare at 5,000 color swatches and combinations, get a headache, my self-confidence plummets, and I go home defeated."

Making paint decisions at the paint store is like grocery shopping when you're starving—not a good idea. There are hundreds of samples in paint displays because you're supposed to take them with you and

make these critical decisions in the comfort of your home, where the color will actually end up. This may seem obvious, but you'd be surprised how many people put themselves on the spot in the paint store and try to make decisions in that distracting environment. They ask the opinion of an employee who has never been in their home, and probably worked in the lumber department the day before. They end up playing it safe and arriving at home with white, beige, or nothing.

We hide behind white because we think it's safe. To compensate for lack of color, we spend thousands of dollars on upholstery, rugs, drapes, and accessories to keep our interiors from looking cold and sterile. You will forever be fighting to make your rooms look warm and inviting if you don't

paint with color! Even museums hire color consultants to advise them on complementary colors that will enhance the artworks and make their galleries less intimidating.

White creates hard-to-deal-with contrast. Dark wood furniture appears darker against white, and rich accent colors and fabrics turn into black holes in a white room. Accessories are left to float in space against white, and we place the burden on them to bring a room together. By contrast, the proper wall color can unite a room, showcase your objects, and work wonders for the environment.

In some exceptional cases a white room will work. If you want a Manhattan loft feel, if you live close to the water and the house is flooded with light, or if you're seeking a postmodern, monochromatic look, then

use white. But keep in mind that there are hundreds of shades of white. The warmer the white, the better the look. If you want a room to be white but not glaring, a pale beige will look white on the wall. It accepts natural light better and is more flattering to skin tones. Make your choice wisely if you decide to go white.

TAKE TIME CHOOSING

At the paint store, select a handful of swatches in a color range you might like. If you're interested in blue, take home all the color swatches in blue shades. Find a quiet moment when you have time to sit down and play with the colors. I start by putting color combinations together that are pleasing to my eye. Rarely do I settle for the first arrangement. I'll let the colors sit out for a few days, walk by now

Choosing Paint

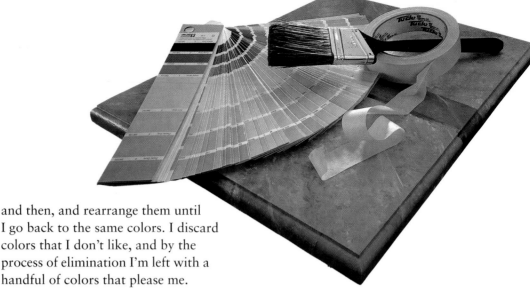

Choosing paint requires two trips to the store. If you know in advance that you're not actually going to be choosing colors on your first trip, you can relax and get inspired. Stop by the store on a Monday evening after work to avoid the weekend crowd. Turn your fear into excitement and pull color swatches to which you're immediately drawn. Take as many paint swatches home as you want. I've been known to take fifty or sixty at a time—that's why they're there. Also available for about $20 is an entire fan deck (right), which represents the complete line of a manufacturer's colors. These decks come organized and indexed for easy reference, but you have to ask for one. Designers carry a fan deck with them at all times, and I've used mine many times on my show.

and then, and rearrange them until I go back to the same colors. I discard colors that I don't like, and by the process of elimination I'm left with a handful of colors that please me.

This process works. Given the right atmosphere, it's amazing how we all instinctively have a sense of color. Without knowing it, we are subconsciously reacting to color every day. It could be a flower, a shade of lipstick, or simply the sky. We're so used to living in a world of color that we take it for granted. By giving the selection process plenty of time, you will feel more secure in the choices you make.

The second trip to the paint store shouldn't be made until you know what you want. Even then, stick to your guns. Don't let the confusion of a busy store get you off stride; don't panic and change your mind at the counter. Feel confident knowing that you've taken the time to choose the right colors. I recommend purchasing paint on a weekday evening so that your valuable weekend is spent working on the room rather than trying to find a parking space.

Now let's talk about color itself. In my traveling road show I select a member from the audience who admits to a fear of color. I hand her a large board painted in an aggressive shade. Then I hand her a piece of molding, a ring of carpet swatches, a bolt of fabric, a picture of a sofa, a picture of a coffee table, a mirror, a candle stand, a small plant, and an up light. Each object represents one of the Seven Layers. The audience is hysterical, watching this poor person struggle to hold everything. It's a dramatic demonstration that if you're scared about using color, remember, there are six more layers to add to the room. How much of that color will be seen, anyway? That rich color is there to accent the pieces you love. It peeks out from behind the pictures, frames a sofa, and cuddles favorite objects. It's the unifying element that ties the room together.

Perhaps the biggest mistake people make in choosing color is not knowing the difference between a background color and an accent color. In cosmetic terms, the background is the foundation and the accent is the lipstick, eye shadow, and blush. If we understand that wall color is designed to show off the accessories in a room, then we can understand why choosing accent colors for the walls instead of appropriate background shades is a mistake.

Here's a cautionary tale: There was a time when jewel tones—deep, royal colors—were all the rage. People

bought into the trend and painted their walls in these bright accent colors rather than in more suitable background shades. When it came time to add accessories, they had no place to go. That cobalt blue vase was the same color as the wall, and rather than adding a splash of color to the room, this accessory simply disappeared.

Yes, you can have vibrant, rich, deep color, but don't build it into the shell of the room. These trendy colors may become dated, so save them for accents in your pillows, drapes, and decorative objects. It's much easier to change a pillow or two than to repaint an entire room.

The goal with wall color is finding the most neutral shade that goes with everything you love, and that works as a background to which you'll add six more layers. Now, when I say neutral, I don't mean beige!

From palest to deepest, every color has its most neutral shade. Find the one shade of that color that is the most versatile. For example, if you've chosen green, your goal is to select the most neutral shade of that green. Look for the one color swatch that is

ABOVE: Color can change from room to room, but be aware how adjacent rooms may complement or conflict. Here cool gray leads pleasingly to warm mustard.

LEFT: Once you've chosen your room colors, pile furniture and accessories in the center of the room so that you won't be distracted or deterred.

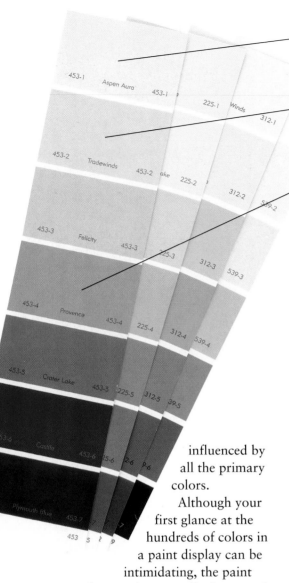

Trim color

Ceiling color

Wall color

influenced by all the primary colors.

Although your first glance at the hundreds of colors in a paint display can be intimidating, the paint manufacturer has actually done much of the work for you. Most manufacturers offer at least seven paint strips in every color grouping. On each paint strip there are six to eight shades ranging from very light to very dark. Each of the color groupings is in a specific order. Find those six to seven green strips, and the most neutral green strip is almost always in the middle. So if there are seven strips, choose the fourth strip. Ta-da! It's that simple. The green strip located in the middle of the group is the most influenced by all the colors. Reread this paragraph until you absorb it.

Now you are holding a single paint strip containing some six to eight green shades ranging from very pale to very dark green. If you've chosen the correct and most neutral strip, the green shades should have a muted, dusty quality to them. The color may look a little subdued to you, but remember it's a background color (accent colors come later). In makeup terms you're about to put on your foundation, with the eye and lip colors to come later.

It's time to pick three colors from your neutral paint strip for the walls, ceiling, and trim. But what color goes where?

On your neutral paint strip there are usually two very light shades, two medium shades, and two dark shades. For the walls, go to the two medium shades on your paint strip. Paint the walls the darkest of the medium shades in a flat finish. I know it looks dark here, but once up on all the walls it will look more like the lighter of those two medium colors. Trust me!

Yes, do paint the ceilings. Introducing rich color on the walls while leaving the ceiling white will make your room look as if you've spread a big bedsheet over it. The ceiling will actually seem lower if left white. If the walls are nine feet or lower, paint the ceiling two shades *lighter* than your wall color also in a flat finish. Chances are it will be the darkest of the light shades. If your ceilings are higher,

paint them one shade *darker* than the wall color. By using two shades of the same color for your walls and ceiling, the light will now reflect evenly throughout the room.

The very lightest color on your swatch is for the trim (moldings, doors, windows, and built-ins); use a semigloss or eggshell. Unless your intention is to create a traditional Colonial look, I recommend keeping the trim color light. This will attract the eye out through your windows and doors, rather than creating a visual barrier. Darker trim colors, including natural wood, can often look cartoonish, while light trim is fresh, crisp, and contemporary.

Once you've chosen your room colors, place swatches on index cards and carry them with you. You never know when you might need to refer to them as you choose fabrics, accessories, and rugs.

The second most-asked question (after what color to choose) is, "How do I deal with color from room to room?" Here's a good trick. In an adjacent room, take the wall color from the previous room and make it the ceiling color. Then take the ceiling color from the previous room and make it the wall color. For continuity, keep the trim color the same throughout. This will provide two different looks, but rest assured that the rooms will complement each other.

WALL FLOWER

Let's talk briefly about wallpaper. There are many who think solid wall color is boring or dull and haven't yet learned that walls are the background to which six more layers of pattern, texture, and color will be applied. Print or patterned wallpaper in the hands of a novice can create a "pattern trap," especially in areas where guests gather. It's expensive to remove, and if removed improperly can result in the need for resurfacing. If you're crazy for patterned wallpaper, isolated areas like powder rooms and bedrooms are the most suitable. Faux finishes such as a rag-roll effect or stenciling can give the room more personality and charm. If you have a more ornate eye, try using a wallpaper border placed at the top of a solid-color wall as a compromise.

If you've inherited existing wallpaper, don't be afraid to paint it. I've painted over thousands of wallpapered walls. There may be a seam or two, but if you're bothered by a line, I think the phrase "Get a life" might be appropriate here. Test the wall first to make sure the existing paper is still securely adhered, and then seal with a stain-blocking primer before painting. Or if you have the money, use a professional service to remove it. If the wallpaper is hiding a multitude of sins and is on securely, find a textured or solid paper and apply over it. Grass cloth and ribbed textures can be interesting.

Back to faux finishing. The greatest mistake I see people make when attempting a faux finish is to have too much contrast between the colors, and the result is garish. The only time I really find it necessary to faux-finish walls is if they are in bad shape and the extra texture will help cover that, or if you're seeking an old-world look. Remember, the idea of these treatments is to add texture to the room, not pattern. Choosing the correct colors is a simple way to prevent ghastly results and assure a subtle faux finish. Select the lightest and darkest of the medium colors from your neutral paint strip and faux finish with these. Since every wall faux finish needs a

base color, paint your room first and give yourself the option of whether you want to proceed. Introducing wonderful color into a room might do the trick on its own. Ask yourself, "Does this newly painted room really need that extra little hoo-ha?" After six more layers, it could be overkill.

If I've done nothing else, hopefully I've persuaded you to lose the white walls. If you've been living with white for a long time, the first stroke of the roller might give you a heart attack. This is natural. Don't make judgments about your color choices until all references to white are out of the room. Only then will you have a clear vision of what the room will look like. Warn wary loved ones, too—there's no sense getting a divorce in Layer One when there are still six more to come. Once you've handled the architectural embellishments, the walls, and the ceiling, it's time for the sixth and final piece of the shell—the floors.

TOP LEFT: This rustic old beam would have looked heavy and awkward against white walls. We painted the shelves the same color as the wall to give them a built-in look.

TOP RIGHT: I chose mustard to accent the rich plum wall color. Split bamboo trim adds a natural touch.

ABOVE: This vaulted ceiling was a challenge. I decided to run the wall color up and overhead, but painted one wall a darker color to add visual interest.

2 Installed Flooring

One benefit of solid-wood flooring is that it can be sanded and refinished like new. This white oak floor is more than fifty years old but looks as if it had been laid yesterday.

OPPOSITE: When it comes to wall-to-wall carpeting, choose a color that you can live with for a long, long time. Take the swatch ring back to your home for viewing colors in natural light.

Whether you choose hardwood, tile, linoleum, peel-and-stick squares, or carpet, the floor connects and completes the room. When I talk about installed flooring, I mean exactly that—a permanent or semipermanent material that is installed from wall to wall.

First, let's get area rugs out of the way. They belong in Layer Four, but I know from experience that many people mistakenly group area rugs with flooring. Don't begin your decorating process by falling in love with an area rug and building the entire room around it—that doesn't make sense. Area rugs usually have pattern and texture not only that are designed to enhance the theme of a room but add color in a layered fashion. Yet many people will take colors from an area rug and use them for design decisions. On a limited budget, does it make sense to spend money on paint, high-ticket upholstery, and accessories to accommodate an area rug, which is easily removed or dated? I don't think so! In wardrobe terms, an area rug should be considered a fabulous scarf that will enhance a wonderful solid-color dress.

Another huge mistake people make with installed flooring is to build detail into a floor that can't be changed easily.

Complicated floor patterns turn what should be the background (part of the neutral shell of the room) into an accent. We go crazy with pattern and detail. A little border here, a floral inset there, a dramatic color here, and a $15-a-tile bead molding there—it goes on and the bill goes up. By the time you stuff the room with furniture, you're not going to see much of that floor. Like rich wall color, it will stare up at you in a strip between the chest and the wing chair, between the area rug and the baseboard.

Unless you are creating a bowling alley or a ballroom, keep floors simple. Don't overdo, exercise the art of restraint, stick to the system, focus on the background, and save your exciting pattern ideas for later. Otherwise you'll spend a fortune and find yourself in a pattern trap with no way out.

Admittedly I'm a tightwad, so I like to work with what I have and save money early. Then maybe later on I can afford that fabulous sofa, or at least rationalize its cost. Learning the art of disguise is a way of prioritizing where to spend money and get the biggest bang for your buck. The idea is to finish the room, and that's not happening if you run out of money in Layer Two. If you aren't rich, at least create the illusion of living well. Then upgrade as you can afford it.

CUSHION THE BLOWS

From the letters I receive, the majority of you have wall-to-wall carpeting. Certain carpets, like pea-green shag, orange indoor-outdoor carpet, and your green-and-blue AstroTurfs, should just be removed! My rule of thumb is that anything that could have been used to decorate an old Howard Johnson's should just go.

But if you find yourself stuck with wall-to-wall carpet that you can't replace, don't worry. By the time you add all the layers, you won't see that much of it. If the color of your carpet is a light shade that you can live with, simply incorporate it into the room as an accent color. Just as with inherited bathroom tile, this trick will give the carpet an intentional look.

If you can afford to replace the carpet, here are a few tips. Consider purchasing your new carpet from a carpet store rather than a hardware outlet. Carpet companies are abundant and extremely competitive, so shop around. You may be able to bargain with the retailer, depending on how much carpeting you order. Most carpet stores offer discounts on remnants left over from big commercial jobs. If you don't see remnants on the floor, ask about them. Some stores don't flaunt remnants, in an effort to steer you toward more expensive brands. These remnants usually wear well since they were made for offices and other public, high-traffic areas. A word of caution, though: these custom carpets will probably not be available for purchase in the future, so it's a good idea to buy a little extra if you anticipate a future need. Often I will use these custom carpets as area rugs and ask the retailer to bind the carpet in the color of my choice.

When choosing carpet, consider three things: color, type of pile, and wearability. If you've already selected your neutral paint strip, then you already have the carpet color. Take your paint strip to the store and match your new carpet to one of the medium colors. How easy is that? Try to keep your carpet color the same from room to room for continuity. I also like matching my carpet to the trim color since it's already a connective element between rooms.

There is a standard rating label on the back of most carpet samples that describes its construction and wearability rating. This industry standard is designed to inform the consumer that the carpet has been through rigorous tests, so flip those carpet samples over and get the scoop. In low-traffic areas, go with an inexpensive carpet. If a room rarely gets used except as a passage to other spaces, minimize the wear and tear with a runner over the heaviest footpaths. If the carpet is destined for a high-traffic family room, then go for at least a medium grade.

Remember that carpet is a background color, so when choosing the

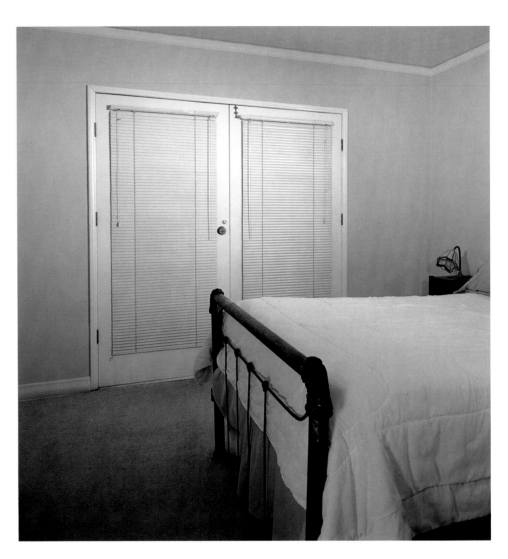

Wall-to-wall carpeting is pleasing to tired feet, but don't forget that it's still part of the background. Take your paint strip to the carpet store and focus on texture, not pattern.

style of carpet, focus on texture, not pattern. Take carpet samples home even if it means leaving a refundable deposit. A carpet sample in a store under bright fluorescent light may look different under natural light in your home. Bringing samples home also lessens the burden of making critical decisions in a busy store.

Also pay attention to what you're getting underneath the carpet. Padding not only is recommended for tootsie comfort but will extend the carpet's life. Contrary to popular belief, thick padding is not always the best choice. Too dense a padding can break down the carpet's construction; a medium

weight is usually just fine.

Professional installation is a must and should be included in the price of your carpet. Get a final quote and pay half of the bill, specifying that installation is guaranteed in the quote and must be completed to your satisfaction. If you know that you'll be laying carpet on stairs, make sure you communicate this in advance to your salesperson before he or she totals the bill, as it usually costs extra. Certain carpets also bend more easily than others, so check that the carpet you've chosen will not be too rigid. Pay the final balance only after inspecting the work, and save any left-over remnants

for future use. For this reason, I recommend sticking with a simple, even texture in a solid color. This will make future repairs a breeze.

If your room is an odd shape and seams are necessary, make sure that the seams are heat-bonded on the back of the carpet. If one piece of carpet is simply butted up against the other with carpet tape, it will eventually unravel. Cats have a field day once they discover splitting seams—they find these imperfections as expertly as a pig finds truffles.

In areas where the carpet ends and a hard floor begins, don't put down an ugly brass strip with nails. Ask specifi-

The floor is in effect the sixth wall of the room. Best to keep it neutral, since there are five more layers yet to be added.

cally for a blind threshold. The installers will wrap the carpet under a tacking strip so that it simply ends without hardware. If you want a custom wood threshold, buy it in advance and have it painted or stained and ready for the carpet layers to install.

Finally, laying carpet is a back-breaking job. Have cold drinks and a tip ready for the installers. It's an incentive for a job well done if you inform them in advance that they'll receive a tip for good work.

WELL-HEELED

The effect of hardwood floors in a home can be grand. Hardwood floors are considered color because wood is colorful, and they have texture that will add pattern to the room. If you don't have existing hardwood floors, installing them is expensive and involved, and I recommend hiring a contractor.

Once you've committed to the expense, knowing where to begin and end a hardwood floor is the next decision. In my opinion, the wood motif should continue through all public rooms, including connecting halls. In an effort to save money, people make the mistake of using several materials in a house: marble or stone in the foyer, carpet in a back hall, tile in a bathroom, and linoleum in the kitchen. This breaks up the continuity and visual flow of the home.

For maximum versatility, I recommend choosing a wood finish as light and warm in tone as possible. Lighter wood floors will go with a greater variety of furnishings than deeply colored floors. Light ash and natural pine will be easier decorating backgrounds than dark mahogany or rich oak. Technology has advanced tremendously in laminated and veneered floor materials, which are easy to install, authentic looking, and remarkably durable.

If your inherited wood floors need

Painted Floors

Another solution for inherited floors is painting. Rather than living with a nasty floor, you can treat the floor as a wonderful canvas for your creativity. When we left our former studio and moved into a new, fully functional home on the backlot of Universal Studios in Hollywood, we inherited the worst dark hardwood floors you could imagine. With hefty start-up costs for the new "Christopher Lowell Show," installing another floor was not possible.

Painted floors are always an option and quite traditional in period homes. If you hate your floors and can't afford the disruption or expense of refinishing, painting provides a wonderful look.

We decided to experiment on our studio floors before simply painting them. With chalk, we drew two-foot squares on the diagonal across the entire living room floor and then taped it off. We chose a checkerboard crackle finish but left every other square in the dark wood we had inherited. The finish required two colors in addition to the crackle medium, so we used our wall color as the base coat and trim color, and selected a buttery cream for the top coat. After four coats of polyurethane, the effect was sensational. Now neatly contained in squares, the bare, ugly floor looked surprisingly beautiful. And we only spent $69!

refinishing, realize that doing it yourself will mean living in a cloud of dust until you're finished. It gets everywhere! This process is indeed disruptive but it can be done; or you can spend the money and hire a floor refinisher. If you've just purchased a home with not-so-great floors, I strongly recommend having them refinished before moving in. Again, consider using a stain as light and warm as possible. Beautifully refinished hardwood floors will add great value to the resale of your home.

For those of you on a budget who crave hardwood floors, here's a less expensive option. Once you lay wood floors, you'll undoubtedly be using area rugs later to bring warmth to the space and they'll cover up at least three-quarters of the floor. Why pay for what you're not going to see? Try creating a wood border, leaving rug-sized squares open. Using this approach, I then install recessed, neutral carpet flush with the wooden borders in these open areas. Now you have the wood look for about half the cost of hardwood floors or wall-to-wall carpeting. Yes, I do have moments of sheer brilliance!

PEEL ME A FLOOR

Another option for disguising floors is peel-and-stick linoleum tiles. My initial motivation for trying peel-and-stick squares was avoiding sheet linoleum, which can be difficult to install, especially around counters and appliances. I know what you're thinking: "Christopher, peel-and-stick—how tacky," but don't be a snob! Technology has made peel-and-stick squares affordable, durable, and easy to handle. I'm not denying that there are some awful designs on the market, but there are also plain, simple, solid

Tile is versatile, forgiving of stains, and well-suited to the kitchen. This ceramic tile mimics old terra-cotta.

colors. Black-and-white tiles on the diagonal can be quite stunning. I prefer laying squares on the diagonal because it prevents the floor from looking like a giant game board. This arrangement makes a narrow hallway look wider and gives a large room flexibility for free-form furniture groupings.

Peel-and-stick tiles are made from flexible material that can be cut with an ordinary pair of scissors. Use the protective, peel-away backing as the surface on which to draw your cutting lines. Remember to patch any holes in your existing floor before laying the tiles. The first row should be laid down the center of your room, since that's where the eye is drawn; then work your way to the edges (I've been known to do three rooms in one day). Once in place, these tiles are there for the duration.

If you're planning to use ceramic or stone tiles, stay away from patterns that will easily date your house. As with carpet, focus on texture when choosing tiles. Today's homes take their cues from the classics: terra-cotta, Mexican pavers, slate, sandstone, Jerusalem stone, and travertine marble. Natural materials are increasingly popular, and specialty tile shops showcasing the advancements in these wonderful new materials are cropping up everywhere. Plan a field trip and get educated before making a selection.

If your floor is cement, explore the idea of acid dyeing. The effect is that of a transparent stain, and the look is pleasing and rustic. Likewise, cement paint colors have broadened beyond basic green, so don't limit yourself.

Whether you install new flooring or transform an existing surface, don't forget that Layer Two is part of the foundation upon which you'll add five more layers. Once the room has been painted and the floors finished, the shell of the room is complete. Live with it for a few days and let the space's character shine through. Give yourself the opportunity to change your mind. It's not a sign of weakness, but of refinement.

3 LAYER Upholstered Furniture

Neutral doesn't necessarily mean beige! Despite rich color, this club chair has a classic design that won't soon look dated.

I haven't the slightest idea of how my taste will change a decade from now. Different times, new styles, fads, and trends come and go, but the world of interior design just keeps rolling along. Knowing and accepting these facts shouldn't make you nuts—unless you are about to pick out upholstered furniture. These professionally upholstered pieces are the ones that will set you back some serious dough, but they should last for at least a decade if you choose wisely. Welcome to Layer Three!

Now don't panic. Just as I've discussed solid and neutral in Layers One and Two, now is not the time to bail on that philosophy. Yet many people do. They think, "I've got solid wall color, solid ceiling color, and a solid textured floor. I need pattern! I demand pattern! I shall HAVE pattern!" Here again, I caution you. If you build pattern permanently into your largest, most expensive seating pieces, it may soon become dated or locked into the room you've styled around it. Trust me, you can go pattern crazy later in the accent fabric layer, but Layer Three is still about building a foundation.

Upholstered and semiupholstered items are considered at this early stage for two reasons. First, they require significant lead time to be ready for your finished room; and second, like the walls, ceiling, and floors, upholstered pieces are still part of the background. They are the basic furniture blocks of your room and should be in a neutral palette; patterned accent fabrics can be added in the next layer.

These pieces include sofas, love seats, club chairs, fully-upholstered side and dining room chairs, settees, and ottomans. In other words, seating pieces that you can't easily upholster yourself. For example, a wooden dining room chair with a seat that you can easily pop out, staple a bit of fabric around, and then pop back in will not be a part of this layer. You'll probably use a dramatic accent fabric for these pieces, and you'll want to change these fabrics as your taste changes. This is precisely why you don't want to put an accent fabric on a large sofa! It can't be easily or inexpensively changed without sending it back to the upholstery shop.

Upholstery choices should focus on solids and textural prints only. I know —boring, right? Right! But remember, there's nothing boring about maintaining maximum versatility and saving

money on an investment that lasts. Now let's go pretend shopping.

Imagine you're in a furniture store and you see an appealing sofa style, but it's not in the fabric you like. Most people would head over to the sample racks and comb through tons of patterns and prints. Don't put yourself through that nightmare. Find a solid textured-background fabric that matches or complements your paint swatch. If instead you are distracted by the hundreds of patterns, this is what could happen ...

LOVE AT FIRST SWATCH

You spot a sofa and fall in love. It's covered with an adorable floral rose pattern. We're talking lots of buds here. This sofa, you think, will look fabulous in your lovely print-on-print room—until you try to move it into another room. Or try to coordinate the sofa with the other patterns in the room. All of a sudden you find yourself in a pattern trap.

If you adore that wonderful rose-patterned print, don't despair. Choose

The most versatile sofa is a simple, cushioned style with straight lines and a low back. This design will never go out of style, and you can build a variety of room decors around it.

a great solid-colored fabric for the sofa's upholstery. Try a pale, neutral shade of hunter green. Remember, neutral does not mean beige. If your paint swatches are on little index cards and with you while shopping (I bring them everywhere), color selection is easy. Make a lovely floral throw and four oversized pillows in your beloved rose pattern. The eye will go straight to the pattern and the solid green simply becomes the background.

A year from now you might move the sofa into your library. Replace the rose pillows with another accent fabric, like a burgundy tapestry, and it's instant hunt club. Maybe you want to move the sofa into the sun room. Replace the burgundy accent pillows with a wide green-and-white striped

accent fabric—instant beach house. Maybe later you'll want a South-western look. Again, replace the striped accent fabric with pillows made from Indian rugs. Instant Navaho. Get it? The accent pillows express the theme of the room and the sofa, and therefore the pillows change, not the sofa. In the next layer I'll show you how to further incorporate accent fabrics into the room. But for now, let's get back to options for your upholstered items that are versatile, classic, and enduring.

Sofas come in many shapes and sizes. My favorite style is a simple, two-cushioned, rolled and flared-arm sofa with a low back and a straight simple kick pleat. I like to add decorative wood feet in case I ever decide to

remove the kick pleat for a more modern look. Come party time, the rolled arms double as leaning areas for guests. A low back ensures that the sofa won't interrupt the view in a room. When you get to the makeover chapters, look at my choices and how I've layered and accessorized the furniture, integrating it into the rooms (see page 43).

When you order furniture that will be delivered later, pay by credit card. Historically, furniture stores go in and out of business faster than any other type of home-improvement source. If you pay the deposit in cash and the company goes out of business, you've lost your money. Pay the balance only after your furniture has been delivered.

I have two rules on how much a

OPPOSITE: OK, so sometimes I bend my own rules! I couldn't resist a dramatic red love seat in this room. But notice that it's textured rather than patterned, and could be used in other room settings.

LEFT: This gorgeous oversized ottoman does triple duty as footrest, occasional seating, and coffee table, and cross-links the sofa with the window seat.

sofa should cost. If you want a sofa that will last almost your entire lifetime, its construction should be of a solid hardwood frame that is jointed and nailed, which will withstand repeated reupholstering. For this, count on between $900 and $1,200. The sofa should be covered completely in muslin so that its "guts" stay contained. Your final upholstery is added over this muslin skin.

If you want a sofa that will last three or four years and you prefer tossing out and buying new rather than reupholstering, you can pay as little as $300. With budget sofas like these, it doesn't matter what's on the inside because it's not built to last. But you should never pay more than $700 for a sofa that can't be re-covered.

Many designers love one hundred percent down feathers in all their upholstery, but I'm not one of them. An all-down sofa sinks too deeply, and guests get stuck and can't get up. Plus, tushie prints remain in the sofa until you bat, pull, pound, and fluff the down into shape. I prefer cushions that contain down around a poly-foam insert. The down feathers stay in place and the poly-foam insert has "memory," so it will automatically bounce back into shape when you get up. This combination will also save you a fortune because down is quite expensive. Make sure that the upholstery fabric goes all around the cushion; if something happens to one side of the cushion, you can just flip it over.

Hand-tied, individual coils are far better than flat springs or batten straps. Flat springs turn your sofa into a trampoline, while hemp batting straps may rot in certain climates. Coil springs, which are hand-tied together, allow the weight to be distributed evenly. This is more comfortable, especially if two people of differing weights are seated at the same time.

When I buy a sofa, I always ask myself if there's anyplace else in the room where I might want to use the same fabric. It's wise to purchase additional fabric at the time of order, because the fabric could be discontinued or a later dye lot may not match it. The amount of extra fabric you order could be enough for drapes, or as little as three or four extra yards to make throw pillows.

You might want to consider ordering a custom slipcover in a different fabric at the time of purchase. This affords an easy, seasonal change from winter to spring and is the best way to extend the life of fine upholstery. For those of you who crave pattern, use it on a slipcover but maintain the versatility of a solid sofa underneath. Expect to pay about $200 for a well-made slipcover that will keep its shape and stay tucked.

Steer clear of the extra little doodads that are available—they rob an upholstery piece of its versatility. Although trims, fringes, tassels, and welts can customize a piece, exercise restraint. These embellishments can earmark a sofa or chair for one room only. I look at a sofa and ask, "By adding these contrasting bits of detail, can I still move this piece of furniture into another room?" I recommend staying away from the little tie at the corner, the gathered kick pleat, the

tufts and the fringes. Keep everything straight, simple, tailored, and classic.

There are many stores that allow you to customize the fabric, feet, and other details to suit your style. If you like a sofa's shape but want it in another fabric, supply your own. Just remember that the yardage will be over and above the price of the frame (about twelve yards of fabric will cover most sofas). With your upholstery purchase should come simple flat arm protectors in the same fabric. Long rectangles placed over each arm extend the life of your fabric. If the only arm protectors the store provides are the dated-looking kind that reach over the front of the arm, simply ask for extra yardage and hem it yourself.

Let's talk about different types of upholstered furniture. As you go shopping for your high-ticket upholstery, know that there are all sorts of fabulous options for seating in addition to the ho-hum sofa and standard love

seat. In my opinion, love seats provide inadequate seating in a living or family room. Think about it: how many strangers can sit comfortably on a love seat? The reality is one, so why have it snatch up valuable space when you'd be better off with two upholstered chairs? Even if you put two chairs next to each other opposite a sofa, you have comfortable seating for two.

Another alternative to the love seat is the chair-and-a-half. It's smaller than a love seat and larger than a club chair. Most come with a big matching ottoman, which I recommend even if you don't use the ottoman with the chair. A chair-and-ottoman combination has often been my answer to replacing that beloved but ugly recliner. These types of alternatives will make for a more unique environment and one that reflects a true designer touch. Here are some other options.

RECLINERS: If having a La-Z-Boy saves your marriage, then by all means, keep it. However, if you've not been out in the market lately, you would be surprised at the design advancements in recliners. On a recent shopping trip I discovered wonderful new recliners, from mission style to ultracontemporary, in which the recliner aspect was not obvious until leaning back.

OTTOMAN EMPIRE: Designers have known for years about this best-kept furniture secret. The popularity of the ottoman is due in part to its extreme versatility. Once the ottoman was relegated to a basic footstool or other bedroom accent, but today it can be the living room's focal point. Surrounded by a sofa and upholstered chairs, the ottoman provides a place for resting weary feet, or it can serve as a coffee table when fitted with a few lovely lacquered trays. The ottoman is also an ideal and portable answer to additional seating when entertaining. It's low and movable and doesn't obstruct views in a room.

If you decide to invest in an ottoman, make sure that it's firm and well constructed. It should have all the attributes of a fine upholstered chair, including its seat height. As a general rule, the lower the seat height, the more casual and incidental the piece. The higher the seat, the more formal it becomes and more applicable for any room. Here again, the fabric of large "coffee-table ottomans" should remain solid and textural, especially in anticipation of trays and other decorative objects like art books and throws that might be layered on top.

Small ottomans can still provide versatile seating but have the option of being treated as a decorative accent. Stripes and fringes can turn an innocent little ottoman into a sculptural element. Just be clear as to whether you want your ottoman to be a part of Layer Three (solid, textural, and grand) or think it works best for your room as a small accent, in which case it would fall in the next layer, where we'll discuss accent fabrics.

SETTEES: The fainting couch has made a comeback! Settees come in a variety of shapes and sizes. They can be sofa-sized and act as a cross-linking device that joins one furniture grouping to another. A backless settee with rolled arms and a deep seat is ideal. Guests can sit on either side and face opposite conversation areas, and if it has a deep enough seat, can sit back to back. The arms still provide leaning room for standing guests. On a rainy day with a cashmere comforter it's ideal for stretching out. Why faint when you can snuggle?

Another type of settee is called a half-back settee. It has one arm and a back that goes halfway to three-quarters down the length of the couch. A half-back settee usually comes in right and left styles. The obvious advantage of the half-back settee is more back-rest area. I recommend these be purchased in left and right pairs for public spaces, but beside a bed one settee can be delightful.

Finally, there's a chair-style settee which has a regular chair-and-arm configuration but with an extended seat; almost like a chair with an ottoman attached. I find these pieces lovely for a bedroom but not practical for public spaces.

PLAYING SCALES

I think it's important to talk about scale here for a minute while you're thinking about what type of seating to purchase. Scale is a powerful tool that can reinvent the very dynamic of a room. It's a tool that can literally disguise a room's proportions. Proper scale can make a room, just as lack of scale can break a room and rob it of its dynamic. It can make a large room seem intimate or a small room seem grand. Poor use of scale is the number-one reason why rooms don't look balanced.

What many designers know about scale is that, when in doubt, go bigger, taller, and wider. Properly scaled pieces in a small room will actually make the room look bigger; the eye is drawn first to a room's furnishings rather than the actual structure of the space. We'll continue to explore scale in the remaining layers, but in respect to upholstered furniture, keep in mind that a few large-scale

pieces in a room are far better than many small pieces cluttered together.

Layer Three is designed to assure that the early investments you make in your upholstered furniture will be solid ones. If you can keep upholstery choices neutral and textured, completing the rest of the room will be a more enjoyable experience. You are ready to mix and match wonderful fabrics without fear of a pattern trap. More important, if and when all those wonderful patterns and florals go out of vogue, the expensive pieces won't. And that is the beauty of Layer Three.

OPPOSITE: A half-back settee upholstered in a rich stripe-on-stripe pattern creates a stylish nook within a larger living room.

BELOW: Keep upholstered furniture neutral and use accent pillows to change the mood and style of a room.

4 Accent Fabrics

Fabric is not just for windows. Doorways can be draped to soften the room's architecture, create privacy, and add a touch of extravagance. Note the coordinating vertical pattern, which visually raises the height of the room.

Mrs. Piffington hires a decorator, Monsieur Jacques, and is the envy of the neighborhood. She begins to dispense decorating tips to the coffee klatch, and claims that Jacques has found this fabulous, rare, and expensive fabric and is building the room around it. In the hands of a seasoned home-decor professional, this is perfectly fine. But in the hands of an amateur, building a room around an accent fabric is a recipe for disaster.

This is where many people mistakenly begin the decorating process.

Yards of trendy patterned accent fabric are permanently built into upholstered furniture, and these costly investments are forever confined to the room for which they were chosen. If there is one point in this entire book that I want you to grasp, this is it! Do not start your decorating process in Layer Four. You risk starting out in a pattern trap, and costly furniture is oftentimes purchased to accommodate this mistake.

Since our choices have been confined to solid-color and textural fabrics, adding the accent fabrics in Layer Four can be a far more enjoyable experience. We can be frivolous, cavalier, and even giddy with pattern possibilities. We can consider those wonderful fabrics that create a theme and bring your room to life, much the same way that a fabulously patterned scarf accents a lovely solid dress. So how do you make smart but lively fabric choices?

Sourcing fabric is similar to choosing paint color. Take your paint and upholstery swatches into the field and find accent patterns to complement them. Since you have already made these foundation color and texture decisions, your portable catalog of color references makes accent-fabric

selection easier. Many fabric stores already have cuttings pinned to the actual bolt of fabric. If there isn't one, simply ask a salesperson to snip a swatch for you.

As you're scouting fabric stores, take a close look at how they've grouped fabrics into collections. A reputable, well-organized store will help you understand how fabrics and patterns go together. Manufacturers create collections that coordinate large prints with petite patterns, and match geometrics with solids. This can make mixing and matching easier. You'll find that the country chintzes are in one area, the upholstery fabrics in another, and the sheers and laces in still another. Some of the chain fabric stores are designed for one-stop shopping and carry a wide selection of home-decor items as well. Some also conveniently offer custom drape and cushion fabrication, which is ideal since you're only dealing with one source. It's still your responsibility to stay on top of these folks and make sure your goods are finished and delivered as promised.

Obviously this hunting-and-gathering process will take time. Give yourself a break and invest the time

up front. Bring your fabric swatches home and spend time with them. When you return to place your order, don't waver. Stick to your guns, knowing that you've spent the proper time necessary to make an informed decision. I know that this selection process can be difficult to visualize until it all comes together, but have faith in the Seven Layers and the knowledge that so far you've chosen wisely.

WHAT GOES WHERE?

One of the most important elements in Layer Four is knowing *where* to use accent fabrics. We've discussed why an expensive upholstery piece should remain pattern-free, and we've examined how simply changing throw pillows can revitalize a sofa. In addition to pillows, use accent fabrics on table runners or the seats of dining room chairs. Lamp shades, small ottomans, even a few stacked fabric-covered boxes might be all that's needed to spread a pattern evenly around the room. It doesn't take much to pepper a space with accents and make the solid background pop.

You already know how to cross-pollinate paint colors, but how do you cross-pollinate accent fabrics? Let's

Keep your upholstered furniture in a neutral palette, and have fun with pillow colors and patterns.

say you're wearing a solid-color dress (the walls and upholstery), and you've added a scarf (the accent fabric). Would you now introduce another color to your ensemble? I think you're more apt to continue accessorizing with colors you've already introduced. Your makeup, handbag, jewelry, and shoes would probably be chosen to coordinate with the dress or the scarf. The idea is to spread that color around your outfit as evenly as possible so that you look coordinated.

A room should be dressed the same way. The accent fabric is designed to pull it all together. Whether it is in a vibrant jewel tone or a floral pattern, *where* you place the accent fabric is the key. To provide balance, your accents should draw the eye around the room at a glance, since the eye goes to color and detail before anything else. If you introduce yellow in the pillows on the sofa, then perhaps yellow tassels or tiebacks on the drapes will pull the eye over to the windows. Add some yellow pillows on the chairs at one end of the room. In the center of the room, place a yellow throw over the arm of the sofa; at the opposite side of the room, perhaps a yellow table skirt. The point is that the accent color is incorporated throughout the room.

This cross-pollination of color is also a great way to unite mismatched furniture. The eye goes to the runner on the table and doesn't notice that the table itself matches nothing else in the room. Dispersing color evenly will make your accent choice look deliberate and definite. And that makes for a well-designed room. Rooms are like people—without a bit of attitude they're wishy-washy and dull.

Another trick that helps unite furniture is mixing up the pillows. Take the two pillows from the chair at one end of the room and exchange them with the two pillows from the settee at the opposite end. Now all four pieces of furniture are integrated and have a purposeful, connected relationship.

KEEP IT SIMPLE

Almost every room in the house has a window, and window treatments are great places to incorporate a good dose of accent fabric. In an attempt to properly honor our windows, often the best feature of the room, we overdo it. Window treatments keep getting bigger, puffier, and so intensely layered that they start to resemble prom dresses. If your windows look like *Fantasia*'s hippopotamuses in drag, tear them down and let the sun shine in. Today the trend in window treatments is simple, subtle, and soft.

The less done to windows, the better. Your goal is to make the windows seem bigger, brighter, and fresher. Accent fabric at the windows should simply soften the architecture and add tailored luxury to a room. So keep the frills to a minimum. Crisp, clean lines devoid of superfluous detail will always stay in fashion. It's the bric-a-brac, ruffles, and fringes that will date a treatment. When in doubt, do less. The art of restraint also defines good taste.

HANG 'EM HIGH

One of the common mistakes made when hanging drapes is not giving the window proper breathing room. If you hang drapes within the window sashes, a foot of gathered fabric on each side will surely crowd the window. Instead, the drapery panels should be outside of the window casing, exposing as much of the window as possible. If the room permits, I always extend the drapery at least two extra feet on both sides of the window, with the left and right edge of each panel just touching the inside of the window moldings. This visually enlarges the size of the widow.

Another common mistake is to hang valances much too low. This crowds the window from the top and makes it look squatty. Valances should simply drop down to hide the top of the window molding. To make the window and room look taller, I always put my rods as close to the ceiling as possible and leave a generous puddle of fabric on the floor. The puddle gives an air of extravagance to a room. Stiff pinch pleats are for motel rooms.

Use your wardrobe sense and you'll find that these little tricks make your windows look taller, wider, and more dignified.

Although windows are ideal places to add accent fabrics, you don't have to choose a pattern. Solid and heavily textured fabrics will also soften the room and still look pleasing. Decide whether you want the windows to be major focal points or part of the background. A textured pattern will blend into the wall or trim color, while pronounced patterns stand out more prominently.

I ask myself, "Can this room handle a lot of pattern?" The answer usually has to do with the room's size. Large rooms can handle more pattern than small rooms. Smaller spaces tend to get dwarfed and busy with too much color and pattern, so I go more monochromatic with small spaces. Try this little trick: When selecting a drapery fabric, step back and squint your eyes. If the print appears more like texture than pattern, chances are it will make a good window treatment.

If you're still not sure, a great compromise is to use a solid fabric and add a three- to four-inch band of accent fabric to the inside edge of each panel where the curtains open to reveal the window. These vertical borders integrate an accent into a room, yet assure that you won't overdo it. You can also add this same pattern to a valance or tieback. If your rods are installed close to the ceiling, these vertical patterns will also further the illusion that the room is taller.

OPPOSITE: To make windows appear larger, hang the curtain rod close to the ceiling and extend the drapery panels two feet on each side. Let the curtains puddle on the floor.

ABOVE: This arched window is a fabulous fake. We made the ledge and molding from plywood, and stapled the pleated Roman shade to a semicircular piece of luan plywood (see pages 66–67).

33

Light or privacy? This window treatment offers both. Natural light pours through the bay window and its sheer valance, but the simple, textured drapes can be drawn at night. The many fabrics in this room work together because the larger items are relatively neutral and the smaller pieces carry the pattern and color.

MORE WINDOW-TREATMENT TIPS

MULTIPLE WINDOW WALLS: Many entry halls have windows on top of windows. I deal with these stacked windows by treating the entire wall as one large picture window. Place long, ceiling-to-floor fabric panels that stretch from the wall to the first group of windows. The next panel goes between those windows and the next set. Repeat this until your last panel bridges the gap between the last set of windows and the opposite wall.

ARCHED WINDOWS: The easiest way to treat these tricky openings is to ignore the arch, keeping it clear of drapery. Where the arch straightens out, place a pole and brackets and extend the pole a foot beyond the window on both sides. This will separate what is now a half circle from the rest of the window. Add two fabric panels cascading to the floor and you're finished.

CORNER WINDOWS: The idea is to unify the corner as the window turns from one wall to the other. Add a pole and bracket, or if it's a breakfast nook, a shelf can be added. One panel goes on the far left, another in the center where the window turns ninety degrees, and another at the end of the window on the next wall. A shelf or simple valance will visually connect one wall to the other, making the two windows seem like one. If you have the space, extend the drapes past the openings to make these windows seem larger.

SLIDING GLASS DOORS: Another place where a wooden shelf and brackets can add interest to the opening is above the patio doors. In between the brackets, place pole sockets and ordinary one and three-eighths-inch closet doweling. Once it's installed, paint everything the same color as the trim. Then, using three panels of fabric, I shirr one on the left, one on the right, and one in the middle where the doors overlap.

This hides the seams, leaving only the glass visible. The overhead shelf adds character and awaits your accessories.

WALLS WITHOUT WINDOWS: Just because you don't have a window doesn't mean you can't fake one. To bring balance to a lopsided space, I often put up the same drapes on a solid wall that I've used on a window wall. I pull the drapes open with tiebacks that match the rest of the room, and where there should be a window, I instead add a lovely framed mirror that pulls the light from the real window over to this dark area. It's an easy illusion that balances a lopsided room.

DOORWAYS: Entrance draping is back in vogue! It makes an interesting transition from room to room. Dining room entrances become more grand, foyers are softened with an added touch of fabric, and living room spaces feel slightly mysterious. Peeking through pulled-back drapes is far more intriguing than seeing everything all at once.

SO MANY FABRICS, SO LITTLE TIME

Now that you know where to incorporate accent fabrics and how to dress your windows, let's talk about specific materials. There's a wide variety of fabric textures and fibers available today. A visit to a fabric store will introduce you to many options, but here are a few of the most popular fabrics on the market.

SHEER: Sheer used to conjure up a very grand, old-fashioned image. Sheers are now available in a variety of colors and prints that are appropriate as accent fabrics. Soft folds of translucent or opaque sheer can add simple softness and romance to a room without overwhelming it. Because of sheer's light weight, it moves when a breeze wafts

though the room. Here again, keep it simple and steer clear of ruffles, pleats, and ties; sheer is at its best as a gentle fold of billowy fabric against a luscious wall color.

CHINTZ: Chintz is a traditional, polished cotton with a slight sheen, like semigloss paint. It's usually most effective in vibrant floral patterns. Chintz is ideal for creating a decidedly English look, depending on the style and use of these fabrics.

TAPESTRY: Until recently, tapestry material was rather limited in its use and confined to decorative hangings, heavy in both weight and attitude. Manufacturers today are printing a traditional tapestry look on lighter and easier-to-work-with fabrics for a fraction of the cost. Tapestry can add a great deal of drama to a room. Just be sure you've got a grand space that can handle it.

CHENILLE: Primarily used for upholstery, chenille is a versatile, durable, and soft fabric that adds great texture to a room. Again, due to technology, chenille is now manufactured in many weights and in both prints and solids.

GOT YOU COVERED

My job is to show you how to maximize every inch of your living space, and the key is creating rooms within rooms. One of the best decorating tools for accomplishing this is the area rug. Since area rugs are heavy accent fabrics, they're introduced in Layer

Four instead of Layer Two (installed flooring), so don't be confused. When layered over installed floors to add texture and pattern, area rugs help to redefine spaces.

As an accent fabric, area rugs can add instant theme. A braided rug is pure country charm, while a wovengrass mat adds an Asian twist. A word of caution, though: An area rug can further the theme, but it can also overwhelm. These rugs should help ground a room, not sink it. A good area rug should have a pattern or texture that can be interrupted by furniture and still work. I prefer muted tones that look more textural than patterned.

If you have light-colored furniture, go darker with your area rug. If your furniture is already dark, try a lighter rug. Contrasting one great element against another is better than having it all blend together. Also take into consideration that an area rug is rarely seen in its entirety once on the floor.

At this point in the Seven Layers, all the difficult decisions have been made and the shell of the room is complete. Your pricey upholstery investments have been protected from becoming dated because you've kept them solid and textural, and your accent fabrics have now brought wonderful color and pattern into the room without overwhelming the space. The door is still open to change as trends come in and out of fashion. I love that!

Non-upholstered Furniture

Now you see it ... We hid our studio's stove and microwave behind the latticed doors of this home-built cabinet. It's a good example of why I call such pieces "workhorses."

The shell of the room is finished, and we're almost ready to display our wonderful decorative items. But where? After establishing primary seating arrangements in Layer Three, you should have an idea of how much space is left over. This space should be devoted to the non-upholstered furniture, or the side pieces, that will add surfaces and storage areas to a room. These workhorses, as I like to call them, can really make or break a room, and here's why.

Our spaces have to work harder today than ever before. We require comfort and function from workhorse pieces, but also demand that they be as attractive as possible. We want our rooms to reflect classic taste, but also to maintain a modern sensibility. Our spaces should help us blend technology into our homes, but also make us feel recharged and connected to our humanity. Layer Five is designed to bridge these needs.

Comfort must come first; everything above and beyond that is a bonus. It doesn't matter how much money you've spent on the sofa, how beautiful the fabrics are, or how gorgeous the wall color is. Without effective use of Layer Five, rooms are uncomfortable because they don't function well.

SURFING FOR SURFACES

Surfaces come in a variety of forms. An old trunk, a bookcase, and a coffee table all combine to make a functional room. It's unfortunate how many people overlook the importance of these surfaces in a room.

Here's a little story to reinforce my point. I'm seated on a lovely sofa and the host offers a beverage. I take a few sips and we toast to friendship. All is well in the warm-and-fuzzy department—until I try to put my drink down. The nearest surface is four feet from where I'm sitting. The sofa is eight feet long, but the coffee table is only three feet long. On this grossly underscaled surface are the obligatory dried flower arrangement, two candlesticks, an oversized art book, a container of potpourri, and a mysterious bauble. So even if I could reach the table, where would I put my drink? With my naturally high level of energy, I find myself juggling ice cubes, a napkin, and the tray of canapés, which I have to pass up because I'm clearly not an octopus. I could have been more comfortable on a budget airline—at least they've got trays! Do you get my drift? Without proper surfaces, the room fails in the service department.

When in doubt about the appropriate size of a coffee table, GO BIGGER! If you already own an underscaled table, visit a retail store that sells stock glass tops. Buy a piece of glass larger than the top of your existing coffee table and lay the glass over it—same old table, larger, better surface.

Your seating should never be more than an arm's length away from a reliable surface. Don't worry about overcrowding. Bodies only require eighteen inches to pass comfortably between pieces of furniture, so think creatively and add appropriately placed workhorses to your seating and conversation areas. If you have to get up from a sofa or out of a chair to reach a lamp or beverage, that surface is too far away.

While surfaces should provide for the family's needs, anticipate the needs of guests as well. Homes without guest space subliminally tell a visitor that there's not enough room. Think for a minute about hotel lobbies. They always feature an abundance of space and are fabulous places to pick up wonderful guest-accommodating ideas. A properly appointed hotel lobby usually features a side table, coffee table, or drink ledge for lingering guests. A hotel's public seating area has to provide function. These same principles apply to the home.

STORAGE SMARTS

When choosing workhorses, keep the focus as much on storage as on design. I've found that most people shop for surface furniture by looking only at design, never considering function. A glass coffee table looks sleek and contemporary but offers no practical storage in addition to its top. I prefer dual-function furniture, like a coffee table with a drawer and shelf to accommodate the junk that usually gets piled on the table. Bookcases are fine if you have an abundance of books and decorative objects. But if

A sofa-high three-drawer chest mingles happily with a contemporary coffee table, and both coordinate with the painted floor. Guests are no more than an arm's length from a surface on which to place drinks or canapés.

Instant Surfaces

Just because the furniture pieces in Layer Five are hard workers doesn't mean they have to be dull. The next time you're about to purchase a table, use your creativity instead and combine found objects from around the house, or visit a flea market. A sofa may be difficult to make yourself, but a table can be crafted from just about anything. It's more about being resourceful and clever than spending big bucks. Try one of these fun but functional ideas.

• A giant wicker basket with a piece of glass on top provides hidden storage underneath and works as an end or coffee table.

• Old flea-market suitcases stacked atop one another combine form and function into one eye-pleasing element.

• Pair an oversized outdoor terra-cotta pot with a round glass top and you've got ample table space for at least three club chairs.

• Four stacks of old but sturdy books can act as legs, supporting a piece of glass, and voilà—a low coffee table.

• Find a flea-market bench and place it in front of the sofa, stacking piles of art books underneath and a pair of candlesticks on top. A bench also works well at the end of a guest bed to hold a gift basket or suitcase.

you need a place to hide the boxes of family photos you've been meaning to sort for the past decade, a trunk or chest of drawers is more practical. A small four-legged side table is better replaced by a small serpentine-front, three-drawer French chest. When every inch of space counts, choose furniture that has both form and function. Your rooms will stay organized and clutter-free when you're ready to add accessories in Layer Six.

I've made the mistake of choosing design over function in the past. The day that I had enough money to purchase my first piece of adult furniture, I chose a lovely curio cabinet in the Biedermeier style. It was mirrored inside and featured thick glass shelves and recessed lighting at the top. I dashed out to the museum shop, bought three wonderful faux artifacts, and placed one on each shelf. Indirectly lit and mirrored, my minimal accessory investment looked like a million bucks inside my new cabinet.

I picked up some mismatched but

lovely china pieces a week later at a flea market. I wasn't sure how to display them, so into the new curio cabinet they went. The plates covered up most of the mirrors and crowded the artifacts a bit, but they looked pleasant under the recessed light. Several months later my grandmother passed away, leaving me all sorts of wonderful silver pieces that also went into the curio cabinet. In three short months, this fabulous piece of furniture was suddenly reminiscent of the cluttered, open shelving of a retail store.

The cabinet taught me several lessons. First, just because you own it doesn't mean you have to show it. Second, it's not what you own but how you display it. And third, there should be as much closed storage in a room as there is seating furniture.

I know what you're thinking. That sounds like an awful lot of furniture for one room, but accommodating all this furniture has more to do with its placement than the size of the room. In my experience, most of you already have enough surfaces, but you're not sure how or where to position them. We already touched on the value of well-placed furniture in Layer Three, but let's review it again with our workhorses in mind.

We know that clustering upholstered furniture around an area rug in the center of a room will make comfortable conversation groupings. These large pieces can often act as anchors next to which you can position a dual-function workhorse. I love pushing a long writing desk up against the back of sofa. It provides storage, a resting spot for accessories and reading lamps,

and the perfect place to sit and write a letter. Similarly, a three-drawer chest pushed up to the back of a sofa and flanked by two occasional chairs is the perfect place to stash board games, candles, and cocktail napkins. It's also the beginning of a new conversation area. Creating these islands of furniture frees up the walls for additional side pieces and storage.

IF YOU CAN'T BUILD OUT, BUILD UP

When thinking about your walls and how to take advantage of the space they provide, here's an important con-

cept to keep in mind. If you can't build out, build up! (You'll read this several times before the end of this book.) A bookcase could span an entire wall and reach up to eight or nine feet in height, but it only takes up floor space one to two feet deep. It's amazing how much stuff can be stored in a wall unit. Using shelves and bookcases for your storage needs leaves other surfaces available for clutter-free entertaining.

Most of us think of erecting shelving units near our seating spaces, but shelves are wonderful at the end of a hall or around a small window. Shelves add warmth to these nooks

OPPOSITE: I designed this coffee table to work both as a practical surface area and as hidden storage. It's really just a simple plywood box covered in caning, wood trim, and antique-looking hardware.

LEFT: This elegant little bedside table is really an upside-down planter wrapped in fabric and gathered with a tieback and tassel. The glass top extends the surface area to accommodate a lamp, clock, and accessories.

Dual-purpose rooms like this home office/ guest bedroom require hidden space and clever storage. Here we surrounded the window with shelves and hip storage containers. A simple fabric panel can be drawn to hide the office items when guests show up.

and crannies and turn a pass-through space into a real workhorse. Love that!

Shelving can also make a difference in a home office, which often does double duty as a guest bedroom. Hidden storage is a trick that transforms a functioning work area into a comfortable guest room. Hat boxes and wicker baskets filled with office supplies look attractive and serve the important purpose of organizing work-related items.

The office-in-an-armoire is another clever idea for keeping a messy office contained and out of sight. They can be costly, but making your own version of the armoire office is quite affordable. Purchase an inexpensive cabinet, add some applied molding, a few pull-out shelves, and an antique paint finish, and you've created a country-looking hutch at a fraction of the cost.

Attractive and stylish storage containers have helped dual-purpose rooms gain popularity. Chain stores specialize in great-looking pieces that hide everything from bills and files to serving pieces and seasonal decorations. Canvas bins, stainless-steel buckets, even hat boxes stacked in a corner are all handsome storage alternatives.

It's important to think about scale and proportion in Layer Five, too. We tend to furnish from the floor up to the middle of a room, but hardly consider the overhead space from the waist to the ceiling. Consider it! Using this space will give your rooms proper scale, and that's a distinguishing mark of a designer room. A few oversized pieces will add scale and balance, drawing the eye to the amount of furniture in a room rather than its size. I've seen rooms in which a tall book-

case and an armoire are placed on the same wall, while opposite walls are left bare. There's nothing on this wall to pull the focus up and into the mid-range and beyond. When this happens, the room seems haphazard and undefined. Who feels comfortable in a room with this kind of energy? Not me!

Every wall should have at least one focal point. If you have a bookcase on one wall, place the armoire on the opposite wall. Now you have two tall focal points on opposite walls, and you've got balance. A fireplace mantel creates mass and focus while a pair of pedestals ready for tall trees (we'll discuss plants in Layer Seven) add height and symmetry to the other side of the room.

WOOD WISE

I get asked all the time about mixing and matching wood furniture. Frankly, today's look is so eclectic that different woods in the same room don't bother me. What does bother me, though, is mixing formal and informal furniture in the same room. A Queen Anne table and a modern Danish cabinet have little in common. Neither piece is in balance and the result is a wishy-washy interior. Extreme opposites work better than kissing cousins. The very formal coupled with the very primitive does work. A Spartan, distressed piece of furniture against rich, elegant fabric has great character. But the "sort-of-informal" with the "kind-of-casual" results in a ho-hum, dorm-room effect.

Use color and fabric to unite furniture styles and create relationships between mismatched pieces. Placing two brightly colored pillows on a sofa and a matching table runner on a chest gives these two pieces commonality. You can also unite different styles of

furniture by painting them similarly. It's an affordable solution for tying together unrelated furniture, and an ideal technique for flea-market finds.

If you prefer new furniture in a consistent theme, make sure the pieces don't match *too* much. There's nothing interesting about a room full of furniture that looks as if it all came from the same showroom. To achieve an English look, every piece in your room does not have to be wicker. A distressed and painted flea-market cabinet paired with an outdoor English bench and a few pieces of wicker is much more interesting.

On my television show I never delve into the history or specifics of antiques. You don't need an extensive, historical knowledge of antiques to create the impression of antiquity in your home. Don't burden yourself with the difference between the

Hepplewhite style and a Chippendale piece. Who needs a degree in botany to pick beautiful flowers for a lovely arrangement? When you style your hair, do you comb it all in one direction, leaving the other side of your head flat and lifeless?

No, you make sure that your hair is balanced everywhere. It's all about symmetry, common sense, and understanding balance, and you already have these skills.

Layer Five is designed for functionality. It assures that the workhorses of the room look fabulous while serving the space effectively as surface or storage areas. If you grasp this layer, you'll not only have a better understanding of how to manage your living spaces, but you're ready for the next and most fun layer of all—accessories. Onward!

Another disappearing act: the office-in-a-cabinet. So as not to look like office furniture, the cabinet was painted to coordinate with surrounding decor.

6 Accessories

A collection of fewer, larger accessories beats a shelf full of dust gatherers. Here we also alternated two complementary colors: the terra-cotta of several rustic objects and the green of majolica plates.

My favorite line in a movie was delivered by actress Olympia Dukakis in *Steel Magnolias:* "The only difference between us and the animals is our ability to accessorize." Now that's a woman after my own heart!

Accessories are the jewelry of a room. It helps to think about accessories in wardrobe terms: Earrings add sparkle to the head, bracelets draw the eye to the arms, and shiny shoes bring the focus down to the feet. Well-placed jewelry adds interest and luster to an outfit, and the same

principle applies to rooms. Brass candlesticks on a mantel, a brass bauble on a coffee table, and a touch of gold leaf on a mirror add eye-catching glitter and together create a well-accessorized space.

It sounds simple, yet after fear of color, our greatest resistance is parting with our stuff. Most people are drowning in clutter, which can create visual confusion, rob a room of its allure, and kill the atmosphere. It's alarming how we get used to having things crammed everywhere! Clutter is like fast food—it's not good for you, but you can't help yourself. It's remarkable how we suffocate ourselves with clutter rather than draw comfort and peace from a few terrific accessories.

I know that many people are sentimental about their stuff. That bowl from a grandmother, the beginning of a statue collection that was never completed—piece by piece these items add up and take over valuable storage and surface space. Streamlining means confronting change, and I realize that this can be difficult. Perhaps there's a piece on your mantel that has been there for the last decade. You may not even remember exactly what it is, but you're loath to part with it. You've become so used to that bauble taking up that particular space that you can't fathom getting rid of it.

Don't be afraid to pare down. If you can't bear to part with a sentimental but not-so-great accessory, try putting it away in a box in the garage for a month. If you really miss it, then maybe it does belong inside. I'm willing to bet that after clearing out the majority of your clutter, you won't miss but a few items and your rooms will be better for it.

In Layer Five we learned how important storage and surface areas are to rooms. In Layer Six we're ready to bring an element of drama to these areas. But now it's time to practice the art of restraint. Let's go back to your wardrobe. Would you open your jewelry box and put all of your jewels on at one time? Not unless the look you want is a tacky Las Vegas lounge act. You'd probably choose one or two pieces because you know that your jewelry should accent and not overwhelm your outfit.

In the closet, this makes perfect

sense. Then why do we completely contradict this principle when it comes to our rooms, where everything we own is everywhere?

MERCHANDISING 101

Proper arrangement can take ordinary clutter and organize it into wonderful still lifes that lend that designer look to a room. I call this proper arrangement "merchandising." I worked in New York between theater seasons as a window dresser for department stores. My job was to move merchandise by making it scream "Buy me!" Many of the tricks I learned from merchandising department stores are tips that I later used on my television show. Merchandising your home is the key to arranging your belongings into groupings that make sense and look fabulous, and there are several basic principles that you'll need to know.

LEFT: Varying the display levels of your accessories lends visual interest. This can be as simple as stacking plates at different heights.

BELOW: When accessories are lifted on display stands or shelves, they become more significant to the viewer. And don't neglect your walls as places to display three-dimensional objects as well as flat pictures.

Flea-market Frenzy

Flea markets are great alternatives to retail stores for finding unique accessories. They differ from conventional retail stores in that it's your responsibility to successfully navigate the maze of stalls with a sharp eye and a keen shopping instinct. If you've never shopped at a flea market before, here are some things to consider.

• Dress down. If you look too dressed up, I guarantee you'll pay more. A sweatshirt and comfortable walking shoes are appropriate attire. I once made the mistake of going to a flea market in my Sunday best. I certainly don't remember any bargains or savings from that outing! Also bring a hat, as too much sun can deplete your energy and concentration, not to mention giving you a sunburn.

• Get there early. You know you've arrived too late if all you see is people walking out with lamps and picture frames. These, according to flea specialists, are the two most popular items. When they're gone, you know the place has been picked over.

• Take cash. Lots of single bills and nothing higher than a $20 bill will give you some bargaining power. I like to take $5 bills, which seem to be the most versatile. If I have a list of items to find, I usually take about $300. This doesn't mean I have to spend it, but it assures me that if I find a true treasure I can buy it.

• Don't be fooled by booth appearances. A few things on a blanket will cost less than a fully arranged booth. The general rule is that the higher the vendor merchandises, the more you'll end up paying, so shop carefully. Many of these booths are simply extensions of retail outlets. If that's the case, you might as well get the benefit of retail services and purchase the items in the store.

• Make a list. Write down the accessories for which you're searching. This prevents impulse buying and makes sure you don't end up with something you didn't want or didn't need.

• Bring plastic bags. Your old grocery bags will come in handy if a vendor should run out. If unused, the bags simply collapse into nothing.

• Drive an appropriate vehicle. Flea-market shopping is usually cash-and-carry, and most vendors don't deliver. Consider borrowing a friend's truck or van if you don't have one and know you'll be looking for a large-sized item. Sometimes a vendor will let you pay in full for an item and pick it up later, but that makes me nervous, especially when I pay with cash.

Remember, the flea-market experience is about finding hidden treasures. The most valuable items are not those that you think will be valuable for resale. The really priceless things are the objects you personally love.

HEIGHTS AND LEVELS: Nothing brings more interest to objects than varying their placement at different heights. A great example of using different levels for display is a buffet table at a quality hotel during Sunday brunch. The tables are arranged at about the four-foot-high level. The food and serving dishes are at various levels, with fresh produce and flowers tucked here and there. If the food were displayed on the table at one level, it wouldn't look half as great and you probably wouldn't want to shell out the twenty-five bucks it's costing you.

Accessories should be treated in the same fashion as a beautiful buffet, but I've walked into countless homes where the accessories look like potluck. These items may have once been beautifully displayed, but over the years, as additional items joined the collection, these homes, like my curio cabinet, simply became open warehouses. Place accessories on the same plane and they look boring, but landscape them at different heights and they're interesting.

Anything can become a lift or a level. In the merchandising business, I even used wood studs from the lumber yard and cut them into various heights from three to eight inches high. I'd paint or cover them with fabric, and suddenly they'd be interesting product displays at different levels. A stack of books with a small object on top, backed by a stand with a decorative plate and a lovely bud vase with a tall single flower, is sometimes all you need. Lifts and levels will always add appeal to objects and impress upon visitors that there must be something special about your pieces if they're displayed so well.

THEMES: Another way to make sense of clutter is grouping items by theme. I had a client who was stumped by an enormous dining room wall. She didn't know what to do with it and wanted my help in furnishing the space. Before shopping, I toured her house so that I could see what she already owned, and I noticed that from room to room she had elephants. This was not a figment of my imagination (nor had cocktail hour started yet). I counted the number of elephants strewn throughout the house, from little ivory figures to medium-sized wooden carvings. I then asked my client how long she had been collecting elephants. She looked at me like I had indeed been nipping into the cooking sherry. "Elephants?" she thought for a moment. "Oh yes, well, I started collecting them many years ago but lost interest."

"I don't know when you lost interest," I replied, "but do you realize that throughout this house you have more than forty of those little critters?" She was shocked. I suggested that we gather all of them together in one room.

We cleared off the dining room table and went to work collecting the tribe of elephants. I had a carpenter make thirty-six identical one-foot-square plywood boxes. We gold-leafed and hung the boxes from floor to ceiling, and on top of each wooden box I placed the best of the collection. We added a track light at the ceiling, and when it was turned on, the display took my client's breath away. What had been unrelated clutter was now a stunning collection and the dining room's focal point. When objects are united into themes, they gain power in numbers and make a wonderful statement.

COLOR: Another easy way to gather objects into appropriate still lifes is to group them by color. Taking an old, primitive bench and placing three pristine white objects on it looks simple, chic, and deliberate. A wooden plate with a cream crackle finish, a large glass pitcher, an old whitewashed finial, and a white orchid plant can be gorgeously grouped together. A small wicker box and an old wooden bowl filled with raffia balls can look very organic and textural. The similarity in color pulls these items together and

Metal pipe and glass shelves from a hardware store have been used to create a dramatic storage and display space in this small bathroom. Glassware, silver-colored sconces, and stainless fixtures add a jewel-like twinkle to the room.

brings uniformity to unrelated things. I've even taken four or five different-colored objects and simply painted them in various shades of the same color. Clustered alongside each other, they look great.

When grouping by color, don't forget about shape. This is very helpful at a flea market. You might pass by an object that has the perfect shape and scale you've been searching for, but you ignore it because of its color. Painting or faux-finishing this little flea-market find could work out splendidly. This is where learning how to faux-finish can save you a ton of money. Adding your own patinas to found objects or things around the house turns inexpensive pieces into great one-of-a-kind objects. It's also a

thrill to transform someone else's junk into your own treasure. If you pay a couple of dollars for an object and hate the results of your handiwork, simply take it to the curb. Hey, you've had a chance to practice your skills.

I encourage you to try shopping at flea markets, consignment stores, and estate sales. These venues are great sources of unique accessories and funky furniture. I know that some of you haven't yet tried this alternative shopping because you find it confusing to sift through clutter to find treasure. You go home defeated and nursing a headache. Here's a great trick. I call it the "gift box" test.

Find a handsome gift box and line it with tissue paper so that it looks just like it came from a great department

store. Take the gift box with you the next time you go to a flea market or consignment store. If you find an object and aren't sure if it's trash or treasure, pick it up and nestle it into the gift box. If it looks like it came from an upscale store, chances are you'll like it when you get home. The gift box test allows you to separate the jewels from the junk, and it works every time.

THE ART OF PLACEMENT

You know how to shop for accessories, and you've collected objects that will complement your room. We've talked about how to cluster by theme and color, and the technique of using lifts and levels. But where do these clusters go in your room?

One way to prevent your accessories from simply being absorbed into the room and looking like clutter is to think about scale. Try standing at the threshold of a room and looking at your accessories. If you can't identify a particular object from that distance, chances are it's too small. Again, clustering like objects will lend the effect of scale. Six identical votive candles around a vase, although small, still read as votives. However, a collection of silver spoons, miniature porcelain boxes, or small carved figures simply scattered over your surfaces become instant clutter. These kinds of collectibles should be confined to display boxes, under glass in a curio table, or all together on a molding ledge to help unite them. Now they'll look important together as a collection.

Medium- to large-scale objects should be placed around the room to accent furniture and architectural embellishments. Like a bracelet that draws your eye to the arm, a perfectly placed accessory can make you notice a certain feature of a room. The top of an armoire, a ledge over a newly installed door or window, a coffee table or sideboard—these areas should be surveyed through your accessories.

Now that your room is beautifully accessorized and surrounded by all the objects that define your personal style, it's time for the final finishing touches of Layer Seven. It's hard to believe that your room is already only one layer away from being finished!

OPPOSITE LEFT: We carried the accessories in this funky martini lounge right up to the wall.

OPPOSITE RIGHT: Objects don't have to be identical to work as a grouping. Color is the unifying theme for this sailboat, contemporary mask, and flea-market boxes.

ABOVE: Fewer is better, and when in doubt, go larger. I practiced what I preached in this living room, which boasts a few well-placed accessories and groupings that can be identified from the threshold of the room.

7 Plants & Lighting

Ah, Layer Seven. The glow of candlelight filtering through beautiful foliage truly adds a designer touch to this room.

The seventh and last layer is finally upon us. It's about plants and lighting, and how to use these two elements to complete your designer look. Why combine them? Plants and lighting work together to create shadow and texture, especially after dark.

BEYOND THE PALE

Thomas Edison had no idea what he started when he invented the lightbulb. Choices for interior lighting are so abundant that a trip to the lighting store can be just as frightening as a trip to the paint store. But don't lose your nerve. Creating beautifully lit rooms is not that complicated. I'll help you explore sources of artificial light that can lift the soul of even the dimmest room.

The greatest benefit I gained from working in the theater was my experience in lighting. On the stage, lighting allowed the set designer to highlight focal points and place less interesting props in shadow. This invaluable experience taught me how to use lighting in homes in my later career.

One important concept I picked up is how important shadow is in creating atmosphere and ambience. Restaurants are a great example. At a fast-food restaurant, the goal is to get you in and out quickly, and the lighting reflects that. Burger, fries, and a soft drink ... bye-bye now! The lighting is typically overhead cafeteria-style, which makes everyone look stressed and sallow. Who would linger here? The point exactly!

The opposite philosophy is used at an upscale restaurant, where you're likely to spend more if you stay longer. The lighting is seductive and flattering and the ambience encourages lingering. Refined restaurants use multiple lighting techniques—up light, back light, wash light, glow light, ornamental light, candlelight—for a feeling of luxury, comfort, and tranquillity. These establishments hope to encourage that extra bottle of wine or that indulgent dessert.

The same principles apply at home. Your lighting communicates to your guests either "The food is gone, so scram," or "Let's have another cordial and get to know each other." And beyond how lighting makes us feel, it's a fabulous aid for those decorating on a budget.

Additional lighting is often thought to be an expensive proposition, but it needn't be. Yet I've seen tremendous amounts of money wasted trying to achieve a dramatic lighting scheme, especially in new homes. Unsure of where recessed lighting should go, the owners turn their ceilings into Swiss cheese. Or they think that adding a dimmer switch means total mood control.

Any good designer knows that "even" lighting is boring. Washes of light, pools of illumination, and shadow set off by the flicker of candlelight or firelight bring a welcoming glow to any environment. It highlights everyday objects, giving them new dimension and stature. The play of light is dazzling when done correctly.

Are you ready for this? Creating a beautiful, well-balanced lighting scheme has seven layers of its own. I like to layer lighting from the ceiling down to the midrange of a room, and then down to the floor. In my seven layers of lighting, there are hardworking lights and purely ornamental lights, too. Lighting doesn't have to be so serious. Sometimes you fall in love with a decorative light source, so just lighten up and go for it!

THE SEVEN LAYERS OF LIGHTING

LAYER 1: FILL LIGHT   Fill light brings the room's overall level of light up to a comfortable level. It's lighting at its most even. When placed on dimmers (as most lights should be), fill light is best accomplished with a few recessed lights. The bulbs, however, should cast a flood effect rather than a focused spot effect. Chandeliers and wall sconces accomplish this because they add an even temperature of light; however, these sources draw attention to the ceiling because the light is focused upward. If you have a popcorn ceiling and prefer not to attract attention to it, add track lighting in place of your existing overhead and use flood bulbs rather than spots.

LAYER 2: WASH-AND-POOL AND GLOW LIGHTS This type of lighting enhances the surfaces of a room. It's easy to identify wash-and-pool and glow light in public areas and corporate offices. The wash of light against a mahogany wall, a pool of light on an area rug, a reflection of light against an archi-

This wine rack is elegantly backlit, accentuating beautiful molding detail and the curves of the wine shelves. Notice the under-counter light that brightens a cookbook shelf.

tectural element all heighten the ambience. In homes, wash-and-pool and glow lights are often used in new and remodeled kitchens.

Eating and gathering spaces use lighting elements to enhance the room's functionality while keeping an inviting feeling. Under-counter lights brighten work surfaces and add a contemporary twist. This directional lighting also allows the chef to cook while preserving the intimate feel at a pull-up bar or conversation pit across the room. Pool lighting can define specific areas in a room without walls. A seating area with a pair of sofas is easily separated from the service-prep area with proper pool lighting.

Glow light is essentially a form of backlight or filtered light. Think of kitchen cabinets with frosted-glass doors. Iluminating the cabinet doors focuses on the material rather than the objects inside. Backlit wine cabinets or opaque partitions such as folding screens and glass room dividers are all enhanced by glow light.

LAYER 3: SPOT LIGHTING One of the best budget-busting light sources is the spotlight. Spotlights focus attention on objects, making them appear special and significant, while leaving not-so-special accessories shaded in darkness. Spotlight those pieces that you adore for their color and detail, and backlight those pieces that you love for their shape.

Spotlights work best when the light is narrow and intense. The availability of halogen lights has made spotlights more popular. When aimed at an object, they throw a narrow, tight beam clear across the room. All you're aware of is the light and not the source. Here again, an affordable option for spotlighting is track lighting. I recommend that the heads completely enclose the back of the bulb to prevent light from leaking up to the ceiling.

Now let's move down to the middle range of the room, where practical fixtures put light at your fingertips.

LAYER 4: TASK LIGHTING Yes, task lighting is a light source used to accomplish a given task like reading, letter writing, or any other activity requiring near and focused light. Table lamps and floor lamps are good examples. Three-way bulbs work in public spaces like living rooms, dens, and family rooms. The brightest setting allows for intense, long-term reading; the medium setting for quick, at-a-glance reading; and the dimmest for an ornamental pool of

Track-Lighting Tips

Track lighting is once again hip. It's relatively inexpensive, and when the track is painted the same color as the ceiling, the hardware simply disappears. I often use a combination of flood, spot, and pin lightbulbs when I set up track lighting, accomplishing several layers of lighting within one fixture.

Most track lighting can be installed without hiring an electrician, and improved technology gives you flexibility for specialty add-on lamps, allowing full and flexible control of the ambiance. In general terms, the more you pay per head, the more intense light and longer throw your bulbs will have. I have found that a midpriced head has the same effect as the higher-priced heads. Choose a well-established manufacturer that has been in business for awhile so that if you decide later to expand your light package, the manufacturer is still around.

I personally feel that many new lighting heads are over-designed and gimmicky. Here again, go with a simpler and unobtrusive head. The light source is less noticeable while the light itself looks more magical.

Remember that with track lighting you get what you pay for, so consider the price of each bulb. Bulbs often cost as much as, or more than, your track and heads. Do the math first, and then add on as you can afford it.

light on a chest or side table. The bottom line with task lighting is that you don't want to destroy the mood of the entire room just to read something.

LAYER 5: ORNAMENTAL LIGHT   When reading isn't required, ornamental light adds whimsy and sparkle while still pulling its weight in an overall lighting scheme. Ornamental light can be as simple as a picture light over a lovely painting, a backlight behind a large wooden bowl atop a sideboard, or even a decorative lamp that is more an illuminated sculpture than a reading light. Ornamental lighting differs from spot or task lighting in that its raison d'être can be purely decorative. The holiday season is a wonderful time to notice ornamental light brightening a lit ceramic tree or a shimmering string of Italian lights around evergreen bouquets.

LAYER 6: CANDLELIGHT   How many of us have rated our company by whether or not they were worth lighting the candles for, and cleaning up the dripped wax at the evening's end? Candles used to be messy, but not since the popularity of dripless candles.

Candles are popular because they add an old-fashioned sense of sanctuary and romance to our homes, while also being the least expensive source of lighting. Everyone looks fabulous by the flicker of candlelight, but my favorite thing about candles is that they don't have to be plugged in! Inexpensive, three-wick candles are available in almost every height and width, making them ideal for surfaces like coffee and side tables. So light a few wicks and treat your guests to welcoming candlelight—they'll know they've passed the rating test.

LEFT: Track lighting from the ceiling and recessed lights in an armoire provide both fill and spotlight above a Murphy bed.

BELOW: Every desk should be properly appointed with task lighting for computer work or reading. Three-way bulbs provide a choice of light level and work especially well in task lights.

ABOVE: Workhorses aren't the only surfaces for lighting. Placing lamps, sconces, and candles at different heights intensifies the room's mood.

OPPOSITE: Even I can't kill hardy green plants. Adding greenery to a room enhances the organic feeling, but if you can't commit to weekly watering, these days fakes are a definite "do."

Now that we've covered the ceiling down to the midrange of the room, let's not forget the all-important floor.

LAYER 7: UP LIGHT The theater again taught me that as much light should come from the floor as from above. If you've ever watched my television show, you know how crazy I am for up lights—inexpensive can lights that sit on the floor and cast light upward. You can pay as little as $8 for an up light or as much as $60. Personally, I have never paid more than $15 for any up light in my house, thank you very much.

Placed under a tree or behind furniture, up lights produce fabulous effects and are the best lighting tool for casting shadow. Filtering up through indoor trees and plants, these babies throw amazing texture on the ceiling, that often uninterrupted expanse that can be difficult to make interesting. Not anymore!

Place up lights in the corners, and small spaces suddenly seem larger. Behind large furniture pieces like armoires, folding screens, and sculptures, the backlight effect adds a dramatic floating quality. All this while showing off that rich wall color. Love that!

FABULOUS FOLIAGE

As I've mentioned, when used in conjunction with lights, plants are great natural shadow-casters by night. During the day, they add an organic and living element to a room. I guarantee that adding plants in your spaces will bring natural energy, color, and fragrance.

Clusters of plants add definition to open spaces and create focal points around which to gather furniture.

An archway flanked by trees makes a grand entry hall. Areas of an L-shaped living/dining room combination can be separated by using the drama of plants and trees.

Don't be afraid to get creative with plants. A dear friend of mine uses plant drama to transform his living spaces. Driven by budget (or lack of), he took a large terra-cotta pot, added a piece of glass with a hole cut out of the center, and planted a tree. In the evening, he used this one-of-a-kind creation as a dining room table. For little money, he provided a unique dining experience for his guests. With up lights below the glass shooting up into the tree, it was drop-dead gorgeous.

If giant trees seem unmanageable or expensive, pedestals make small trees appear twice their size at half the cost. Take a pair of small palms and place them at opposite ends of a long table or writing desk that's pulled up to the back of a sofa. It's dramatic and intimate, and separates one sitting group from another. It also adds scale to an environment.

I hear a lot of you saying, "I love trees but they hate me." Here's a confession: I, too, do not have a green thumb. But there are tricks that give the impression of greenery without having to worry about your foliage dying after the first month. I like flowering plants in my home, but the minute they see me, they drop their petals. If I thought I'd recommend fake plants or flowers in the home ten years ago, I'd have jumped off a cliff. However, artificial plants and flowers are so authentic-looking today that the illusion is destroyed only by the touch. Be forewarned, though: the more real it looks, the higher the price. But if you consider the price of a $60 orchid

and multiply it over a few years, it's easy to rationalize buying the best fakes you can.

The biggest mistake people make when buying plant fakes is choosing outrageous color. You'd be surprised at how few neon blue carnations actually bloom on this planet. Another mistake folks make is combining too many varieties. Buy simple flowers in natural colors. Since I can take care of ivy and other hardy green plants, I like to find big leafy, oversized plants and stick artificial flowers with long stems down into the soil. This combination of live and artificial helps sell the idea that the blossoms actually grew out of the pot.

TREE HUGGER

There are good-looking artificial trees out there, too. Manufacturers often sell artificial trees in cheap containers that scream "fake." The cheap brass pot or the conventional wicker basket just doesn't work for me. I have a fake braided fig tree in a guest bedroom. I took the tree out of its original container and placed it in a real terracotta pot with moss. I also took off a few leaves and scattered them on the moss. It looked as though the tree was dropping its leaves. After adding a spot and an up light, it looked great. Every guest is amazed at how long it took them to figure out that the foliage was fake.

With both lighting and plants, the more prepared you are, the less money you'll spend. When I go to a lighting store, I make sure I bring photos of the rooms for which I need fixtures. The same applies to your trip to the artificial-plant store. Rows of trees and colors can be distracting. Take measurements of the area you want to fill with a tree or plant, and bring those swatches with you to coordinate interior and accessory colors with the flowers you might like.

The seven layers of lighting, combined with plants, can transform even the most ordinary room into something special. But without good lighting, even the most extravagant environment will look dull and uninteresting at night. Now go forth and decorate!

HERE'S WHERE WE PUT THE THEORY of my Seven Layers of Design into practice with nine typical rooms. These spaces have many of the same problems—and opportunities—as the rooms in your home. We'll start with a "before" photo, then I'll walk you through the "during" process, applying the Seven Layers as we go. We'll end each makeover with a dramatic "after" photograph, and a recap of how we tackled the room.

First, a few tips to help start your own creative wheels turning. Browse through magazines, books, and catalogs. If a room speaks to you, tear out the page and shove it into a big envelope. Train yourself to really look at a photograph. Sometimes you might hate most of the things in the room, but a background color or detail might really appeal to you. If it's a window treatment, you might not like the design, but what about the fabric? Make notes of why you liked the room or element on a sticky note, or staple a note to the picture to make sure it doesn't get separated. All year long my staff and I go through hundreds of magazines, catalogs, and books. If we don't label, we forget why we chose the photo.

Sometimes the color of a ribbon, the blush on a piece of fruit, the texture of a clay pot, or the pattern around a piece of china will inspire you. So don't just look at home magazines when in fact you're training yourself to find inspiration from everything around you. You're developing your artistic eye. An invaluable aid is a Polaroid or disposable camera. I have one with me at all times. When I'm at a store, at someone's house, or even out for a nature walk and I see something I like, I take a reference photo of it.

Stuff the envelope until you can't get another thing into it and don't peek until the envelope is full. You'll find upon opening the overflowing envelope that the most amazing thing has happened. You now have an eye-pleasing and coordinated collection of colors, fabrics, furniture, and accessories to take with you to the home store. No longer will you suffer from overwhelm when faced with all those paint chips and fabric swatches.

Begin this process today and continue until you've finished this book. I'll show you how to arrange the materials into categories that correspond to my Seven Layers of Design. Now let's tour some real-life rooms …

Living Large

The Seven Layers transform a living room

BEFORE

Nobody does casual living better than Californians. But no matter where you live, there are elements of this beautiful living room that you will love. You'll find it eclectic yet casual and comfortable, and that's what the California style is all about. Now let's see the Seven Layers in action.

The Spanish style, one of the earliest influences on Southern California architecture, is felt throughout this living room. Starting with a beautiful arched window that would become a focal point of the room, we also found Spanish influence in a few inherited tiles on the fireplace hearth, another focal area. In my sketch for the room, I imagined refacing the front of the fireplace with new Spanish tiles to lend an old-world yet modern look. Just above the tile I pictured a two-tiered mantel where now there was one. This would double the display space for antique plates, decorative bowls, and candles, and maybe a plant or two. The European influence would make the fireplace come alive.

Another thing Californians do so well is to mix and match a variety of cultures. For a conversation grouping on one side of the room, I sketched an English rug underneath two identical, overstuffed club chairs. We would find two wrought-iron pedestals and top them with glass to add yet more Spanish flair, and put a decidedly Spanish wrought-iron lamp on the table.

Californians love to entertain, and this makes seating very important. In our living room, I envisioned a backless settee and a large sofa flanking the fireplace. The settee would serve as the linking piece between the conversation grouping near the arched window and the fireplace grouping. People could sit on either side of the settee and enjoy the view of the window, or talk with guests seated around the fireplace. Over on the wall near the entrance, we would place two reproduction Spanish chairs on either side of a fabulous mirror that not only reflects the room, but pulls light from the opposite side.

Look at that beautiful arched window and all that natural light! But, hmmm ... that sloping fireplace might be awkward, and the room's rectangular shape could make seating and conversation difficult. My solution was to break up the room into several seating areas, linked by a backless settee. Simple architectural embellishments will coordinate the French doors with the arched window.

California's wonderful weather invites you to bring the outdoors in. The French doors on either side of the fireplace can be whisked open to the patio, adding to the versatility of the space. Above each door we'll build a plywood arch covered with a plasterlike finish and painted to match the walls. The arches will balance the doors with the room's arched window. Using the same beautiful warm chenille fabric panels I picked for the window, we'll put up panels on either side of the doors and inside the arches to unite the space.

If you live in Southern California, you already know this style. But for those of you who don't, take your cues from these photos. Beautiful, overscale furniture,

After the preliminary sketch comes fun with swatches. Begin with your color palette, then start piling on the goodies: fabric swatches, hardware, tiles, even clippings from catalogs or snapshots of your own furniture.

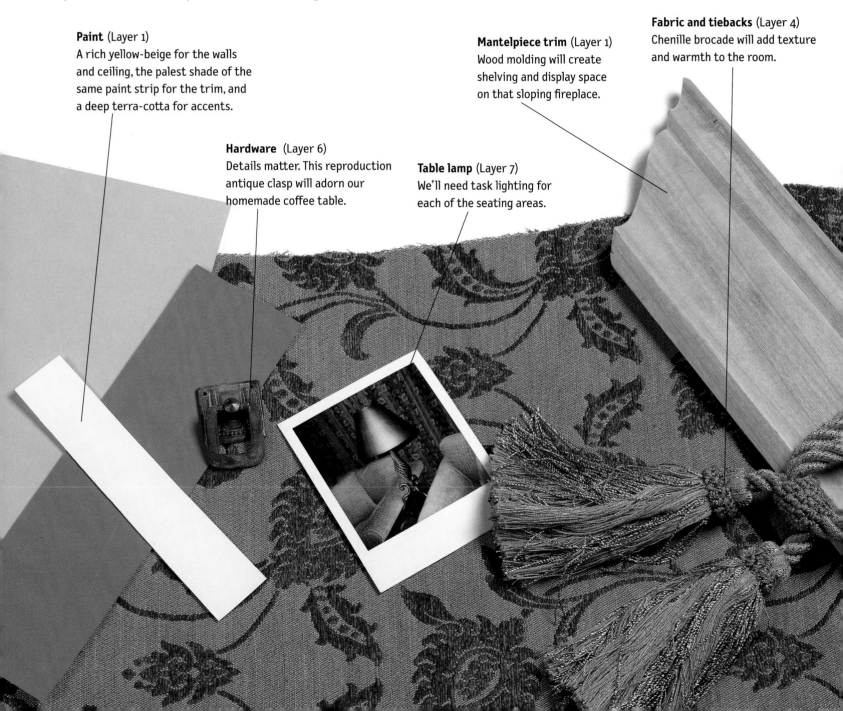

Paint (Layer 1)
A rich yellow-beige for the walls and ceiling, the palest shade of the same paint strip for the trim, and a deep terra-cotta for accents.

Hardware (Layer 6)
Details matter. This reproduction antique clasp will adorn our homemade coffee table.

Table lamp (Layer 7)
We'll need task lighting for each of the seating areas.

Mantelpiece trim (Layer 1)
Wood molding will create shelving and display space on that sloping fireplace.

Fabric and tiebacks (Layer 4)
Chenille brocade will add texture and warmth to the room.

With simple, off-the-shelf wood molding we created not one but two mantelpieces over our Spanish-style fireplace. The arches over the French doors were made from two semi-circular pieces of plywood covered with Flexall to imitate the room's plaster walls.

casual but elegant accessories, and a mix of cultures all combine to bring the California lifestyle into any home. Let's take a look at how we built the living room layer by layer using my Seven Layers of design. Remember: these layers are designed to keep you on budget and out of overwhelm.

LAYER 1 • **Paint & architecture**   First, let's look at the architectural elements of the room. The Spanish-influenced fireplace was somewhat charmless. It had a strange, backward slope up to the ceiling, and there was no mantel. The hand-plastered surface was fabulous, but what good is it if you don't have a place to put your stuff? A big picture hung over the fireplace would have looked awkward against that slope.

So we decided to create a two-tiered mantel with the first tier built about twelve inches above the fireplace opening. This mantel was six inches deep and extended six inches back to the wall. Because we wanted even more display space, we built a second tier at the same height as the embellishments over the French doors on either side. Both mantelpieces were made as simple pine shelves accented with molding. They have turned an innocuous, blah fireplace into a stylish focal point. Love that!

Embedded in the fireplace's hearth were some very interesting antique Spanish tiles that dated back to the 1920s when the house was built. Using the tiles as our inspiration, we refaced the fireplace below the first mantel with Spanish-style tile in a mottled green. The grout matches the background color of the walls and ties everything together. The tile work on the fireplace is part of the shell of the room, so it fits into Layer One. If you can't afford tiles, a stencil would do the same thing. Apply a couple of coats of polyurethane and you're in business.

Next to the huge arched window in the room, the French doors appeared some-what small in scale. To beef up the appearance of these doors, we created an arch above each door that extended two feet above it. Two pieces of three-quarter-inch plywood were cut into half circles and sandwiched together, then attached to the wall. We covered the arches with Flexall, a plasterlike compound that matched the hand-plastered walls of the room. Then we added a ledge along the top of each door at the same level as the upper mantel. The ledge not only added yet another display space, but also concealed a cup and dowel used to hang accent fabric, adding even more volume to the French doors. Now the doors are symmetrical and balance the scale of the arched window.

Time to paint! For the walls, we picked a really delicious color. It's kind of a buttery beige that we also extended onto the ceiling. For the trim, we chose the same color, only it's about twenty-two million shades lighter. This color was used over all our architectural embellishments, except the arches over the French doors. We painted these the same color as the walls to make them appear as a sculptural element rather than as part of the trim.

Remember: if you're living with white walls, you're fighting to get color and warmth into your room. Californians love color, and we wanted to include a bright accent color in the room. So we painted the entry wall next to the foyer a brilliant terra-cotta. What can I say? It looks fabulous!

LAYERS 1 & 2
Paint & architecture • Installed flooring

The room has warmed up with our paint and trim, and the arches over the French doors have become a pleasing architectural element. We found a few lovely antique tiles in the fireplace hearth, and these inspired us to tile the entire fireplace surround *(left)*.

LAYER 2 · Installed flooring   Installed flooring includes hardwood floors, marble, tile, and wall-to-wall carpeting. Often it's easy to forget about these surfaces, but we consider flooring the sixth wall of the room, and you should, too!

Our hardwood floors were in fairly good condition. They were screaming for area rugs, but that comes later, later, later. The floors complete the shell of the room. Before making a mad dash out to shop, live in the environment for a little while with your new paint color, architectural embellishments, and flooring in place and let them talk to you. You'll find that the room begins to take on a character all its own.

LAYER 3 · Upholstered furniture   Layer Three includes all of the large upholstered furniture in the room. This is where you're going to start spending some money. By the time you get to this layer, you're ready to go to the store, where you're bombarded with hundreds of patterned-fabric choices. You can pay anywhere from $700 to $7,000 for a sofa. But when you select one in a solid color, this piece can last a lifetime. Remember to keep the fabrics neutral. Now, neutral doesn't mean beige. It can be any solid color or any textural fabric.

For this living room we chose a big, fluffy, oversized honey-colored chenille sofa. We placed it in the center of the room, perpendicular to the fireplace. On the other side of the fireplace, facing the sofa, we added a backless settee. We used this as the cross-linking device for our fireplace furniture grouping, with one conversation area near the arched window and another by the entry wall. The settee was done in a monochromatic peach damask fabric with matching pillows. What's great about the settee is that two people can sit on one side while two more can sit on the other side, almost back to back. Without having their view blocked, guests sitting on the sofa can still enjoy the vista through the arched window. And they can talk with guests sitting by the window and still include guests on the settee. What's even better is that you can recline. I love that! Every good home needs a fainting sofa!

We created a wonderful sitting area near the arched window by placing two matching upholstered club chairs side by side. They are lined up directly in front of the window, not at an angle. We covered them with a herringbone pattern that is still neutral. Between the chairs and the settee, we've used two ottomans done in a lovely leopard pattern, adding theater and drama to the space. These pieces are a perfect example of what I call textural yet neutral. The ottomans in this layer are considered high-ticket upholstery items, because even though they are small, they are pieces you wouldn't consider upholstering yourself. A little side chair (like a dining room chair where you can pop out the seat, change the fabric, and stick it back on) wouldn't be part of this layer. That comes later.

Behind the sofa, we have two more ottomans and a pair of reproduction Spanish chairs. We have plenty of comfortable seating in the room that's all neutral and textural. The upholstery could be purple—as long as it's not purple plaid.

ABOVE: Keep those big-ticket items neutral! We'll be able to live with this classic overstuffed sofa for years, long after an English hunting print or jewel-box color has come and gone.

Upholstered furniture

Remember, by changing the accent fabrics, you can change the attitude of the room. The upholstered furniture in Layer Three is intended to endure the test of time, which is why we spend more money here.

LAYER 4 · **Accent fabrics**　Adding accent fabric to your room can be a pleasurable experience if you've kept your high-ticket upholstery items neutral. These are the bright colors that bring a room to life. We've done ours in a peaches-and-cream combination as a base color. Now it's time to have fun with some really cool stuff.

　　Starting with the pillows on the sofa, we chose two different Southwestern prints, introducing the colors of rust, brown, a little pink, and blue into the room. Over on the settee in the middle of the room we draped an old Mexican rug as a

First we placed our sofa with a good view of both the fireplace and the arched window. Then we positioned two club chairs and ottomans by the window. A beautiful backless settee ties together the room's two main conversation areas. Now imagine the room without this linking element—you and your guests would have to wave to each other from across the room!

61

throw across the arm and seat. Even though their design is different from the pillows', the color combinations are pretty much the same. Now the sofa and settee tie together beautifully. Your eye goes to the accent color on each piece. The upholstery simply becomes background.

Next, on the settee in the middle of the room we put a pillow in a cinnabar color. It matches the shade of the paint on the entry wall behind the two Spanish chairs. Way over on the other side of the room, we added two more pillows to our upholstered club chairs. What have we done? We've allowed you to view the entire room. You can look from one end to the center to the other end. You can completely survey the room just by using the accent colors as your visual cues. We've cross-pollinated the room and married all of the mismatched furniture. It all seems like one, because the eye always goes to color. Remember, when adding an accent color to a room, make sure you spread it around evenly. Accent colors can also be changed seasonally for a spring-summer or fall-winter look.

Window treatments give us another opportunity to add wonderful accessory fabric to a room. This was the perfect spot to solve some tricky window problems. It's easy to overdo arched windows so that they look like great big prom dresses. If you put a big medallion in the center, and shirr fabric all around, what have you done? You've lost the window. Simple, clean lines of fabric are all you need. Our huge arched window lets a lot of light into the room. We deliberately left the top of the arch open. And why not? No one is going to see in way up there. And if you have lovely foliage outdoors, show it off.

We simply put a rod across the center just about where the arch begins to straighten out, and we added a beautiful chenille brocade fabric. Its weight lets it drape nicely and fall beautifully to the floor. We painted the rod black and put two simple wooden finials, also painted, at the ends. It's big, it's beefy, and it works. And it also ties into the Spanish influence in the rest of the room. More important, we added rings to the top of the fabric panels that allow you to easily open and close them for privacy. We can tie back the fabric panels during the daytime to open up the view of the entire window. Very pretty.

ABOVE: Drawn fabric panels invite us from the dining room into the living room. The patterns may change from room to room, but color is the linking element.

OPPOSITE: Fabric plays a major role in this room. Drapes, panels, and pillows add warmth and texture. The semicircular panels above the French doors, which match the chenille panels, were simply stapled in place.

We used the same chenille brocade fabric in a rich pumpkin color to dress the French doors on each side of the fireplace. Remember back in Layer One, we added plywood arches and a ledge over the doors to bring them into scale with the large arched window. The ledges are now at the same height as the curtain rod we hung on the arched window and the upper fireplace mantel, drawing the eye all around the room. Keeping the horizontal angles the same gives a lot of harmony to a room. These doors now have the same presence as the window. We added a pole and drape under each ledge and hung fabric panels on both sides of the French doors, then secured them with matching tiebacks. To simulate a fan light

Accent fabrics

with Roman shades over each set of doors, we stapled pleated fabric to a semicircular piece of plywood (see pages 66–67).

Another way to incorporate fabric into the room is by using area rugs. I consider them fabric—they're just a little heavier and you walk on them. Over in our conversation area, we placed a wonderful English area rug under the club chairs and ottomans. We used a slightly different English pattern under the coffee table near the fireplace. The use of area rugs defines both the spaces to make wonderful furniture conversation groupings. Neutral background colors and fabrics will allow you to have a blast with colorful accent fabrics. Use your imagination. If you get tired of Navajo, pitch it.

Well-placed accessories and two table lamps in front of this tall mirror double the effect without diminishing important surface areas. A guest could sit comfortably in one of the Spanish chairs and still rest a drink on the table.

LAYER 5 • **Non-upholstered furniture (workhorses)**   I don't care how beautiful your rugs are, how fabulous your accessory fabrics, or how wonderful your sofa. If you don't have workhorses in the room, it doesn't work. Workhorses—what does that mean? These are the coffee tables, side tables, hutches, storage cabinets, the surfaces on which we live—and inside which we hide our necessary clutter.

We built a great big coffee table that we placed between the sofa and settee in front of the fireplace. What I don't like to see in a room is a little coffee table with a little nut dish and a little bowl of potpourri and a couple of candlesticks. There's no place to put anything down! These surfaces are as much for your guests as they are for you. This oversized coffee table makes the area work. By placing it at arm's length from the furniture, the table is within easy reach for drinks, snacks, magazines, or as a place to put up your feet. We designed our table to look like an old steamer trunk accented with distressed leather and covered with caning that was stained to give it an aged appearance. We trimmed the piece with wonderful leather straps and fabulous brass fittings. All the clutter is inside. I think that's so clever.

Whenever you add a tray to an ottoman, it becomes a workhorse, too. We put a tray on top of one of the ottomans near the club chairs. This neat trick turns seating into surface. Between the chairs, we laid a piece of glass on top of a couple of pedestals. Now it's an area where we can put a lamp, a tchotchke, or more important, a beverage.

On the other side of the room, between the two Spanish chairs, we placed a long black table. As a separate ledge underneath, we have an old trunk. Right behind the sofa we placed a great big pedestal. There's an opportunity to bring some plants into the room, but that's later.

LAYER 6 • **Accessories**   Once the high-ticket upholstery items are arranged, the fabrics are in place, and the work surfaces are defined, it's time to accessorize. A word of caution here: little tiny accessories can be like room dandruff. If you stand at the threshold of your room and can't identify an object on a table across the room, it's too small. Keep most accessories large in scale.

Pictures are accessories, too, and we hung two small pictures in a Spanish motif, one above the other, between the French doors and the wall with the arched window. On the terra-cotta wall we hung a huge mirror. Yes, a mirror is an accessory, as is anything that adorns the walls. On one side of the mirror we hung a beautiful watercolor; on the other side we hung two primitive black plates. The table underneath is clustered with old boxes and other cool stuff that looks like something's going to happen. We placed a large jardiniere (ornamental plant stand) on the pedestal behind the sofa.

Our double-tiered mantel offered some fabulous opportunities to create focal points in the room. On the upper tier we placed a majolica dish on a small primitive box. On the lower ledge we used a big Moroccan bowl. Size is everything. We kept the scale of these nice and big. And for symmetry we placed jardinieres on each side. They're piled with lemons and limes, which look great. And we still have some bare spots that we've left for the next layer.

LAYERS 5 & 6
Non-upholstered furniture • Accessories

That wonderful coffee table—really a simple plywood box covered with mail-order caning—anchors the main seating area. Two Spanish portraits stacked on the wall balance the oversized bowl on the mantelpiece, which is in turn echoed by a smaller bowl on the upper mantel. Celadon jardinieres filled with lemons and limes add further balance to the fireplace.

Faux arched window

We needed to convert a set of double doors into a Spanish theme, and bring them more in scale with the large arched window in the room. By adding this arch over the doors, it created the illusion that they are much taller than they really are. They also appear to have an arched window over the top that we intentionally covered with a faux Roman shade. The ledge, which extends the width of the doors, also gives us a place for accessorizing and display.

what you'll need . . .

Measuring tape	1½-inch finishing nails	Scissors
Straightedge	Closet doweling and pole sockets	Marker
One 4 × 4-foot sheet of ¾-inch plywood	Flexall	Fabric double the height of the arch
One 4 × 4-foot sheet of ¼-inch luan plywood	Trowel	Staple gun
Power saw	Metal L brackets	Wood screws
Hammer	Jigsaw or coping saw	Sandpaper
	Kraft paper	Wood filler

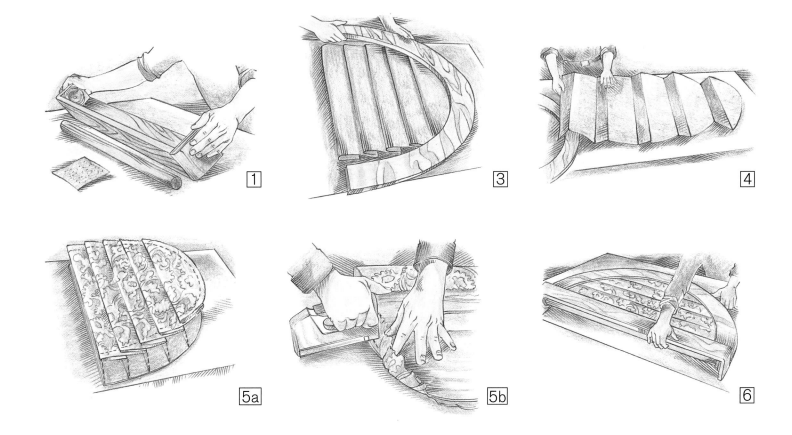

1 First, construct the ledge by measuring the width of the window and adding 6 inches. Make a three-sided box from ¾-inch plywood to this extended width, and 4 inches deep. Nail on two end pieces measuring 4 inches by 4 inches. Add a top shelf. Mount closet doweling cups on the inside of the endpieces. Sand all the edges until they are slightly rounded. To get a plaster effect, spread a thin coat of Flexall on the outside of the ledge using a trowel. Let dry, then mount the ledge to the wall over the window using metal L brackets.

2 Using a jigsaw or coping saw, cut a 4-inch wide arch from ¾-inch plywood the width of the window and the desired height. Sand the edges. Coat with Flexall and allow to dry. Paint the arch and the ledge to match or contrast with your wall color. Let them dry completely.

3 To make the Roman shade insert, fold a piece of kraft paper in 4-inch pleats with 1½-inch overlaps. Place the plywood arch over the pleated paper and cut the paper arch 2 inches larger than the plywood arch.

4 Unfold the paper and use it as a pattern to cut out the fabric. Cut a piece of ¼-inch luan plywood slightly larger than the inner plywood arch.

Draw horizontal lines on the luan 4 inches apart to indicate the pleat lines.

5 Pleat the fabric following the paper pattern. Line up the pleats with the drawn lines on the luan (a). Starting with the bottom pleat, staple the fabric to the luan along the lines. The staples will be hidden under the overlap of the next pleat. Turn the fabric edge to the back of the luan and staple it all around (b).

6 Screw the pleated shade to the wall above the ledge, hiding the screws under the pleats. Then screw the wooden arch to the wall on top of the pleated shade. Touch up screws with filler and paint.

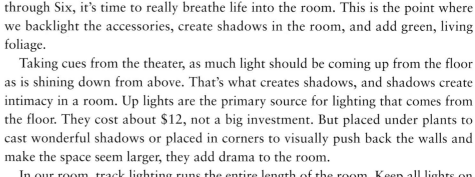

'*Keep your accessories large in scale so that they won't disappear into the room.*'

LAYER 7 • **Plants & lighting**   Once you've successfully navigated Layers One through Six, it's time to really breathe life into the room. This is the point where we backlight the accessories, create shadows in the room, and add green, living foliage.

Taking cues from the theater, as much light should be coming up from the floor as is shining down from above. That's what creates shadows, and shadows create intimacy in a room. Up lights are the primary source for lighting that comes from the floor. They cost about $12, not a big investment. But placed under plants to cast wonderful shadows or placed in corners to visually push back the walls and make the space seem larger, they add drama to the room.

In our room, track lighting runs the entire length of the room. Keep all lights on dimmers so you can control the volume of light from lamps. They're called task lights because they are conveniently located near furniture so that you can sit back and read a book. That's pretty cool. We placed one pair on either side of the mirror, and another pair next to the settee and the sofa.

Finally, there is the warm flicker of firelight. When the fireplace is lit, we have wonderful warmth coming from one side of the room. More important, we have placed candles throughout the room. Candles don't cost a lot of money and they don't need to be plugged in, so they can go in out-of-the-way places where you normally couldn't run an extension cord. We have three great big candles running the length of the coffee table. We added two candlesticks to the lower mantel between the centerpiece and the jardinieres, and another set of candlesticks on the upper mantel. Together they cast light from the hearth to the ceiling.

As a finishing touch, we illuminate large-scale plants with up lights to complete the effect. We added a large palm on a pedestal in the corner by the arched window. Trailing ivy cascades over the upper tier of the mantel. Small up lights illuminate both the majolica piece and Moroccan bowl displayed on the mantel.

There—you've seen the Seven Layers of design in practice. The same principles apply to you in your own home. Wouldn't it be great to say, "I completed this room, it's an incredible reflection of my own personality, and I've got money to spare." *You can do it!*

Lighting brings the other six layers to life. And in this room we have lighting in its many forms. Candles provide light where electric cords would be awkward. Sconces visually elevate the ceiling. Floor and table lamps provide task lighting for reading and conversation.

LAYER 7

Plants & lighting

Here's my recipe ...

LAYER 1 • Paint & architecture Deep, warm walls and light trim set the tone for this room. The same pale trim color will carry through other rooms of the house, connecting them visually. We painted the embellishments over the French doors to match the walls, giving them a more sculptural feel.

LAYER 2 • Installed flooring We were lucky to inherit a hardwood floor in good condition. We simply cleaned and waxed it in anticiptation of adding area rugs in Layer Four.

LAYER 3 • Upholstered furniture We created not one but three seating areas. By the window we placed two club chairs and ottomans. At the other end we located our overstuffed sofa. In between a backless settee links the two conversation areas.

LAYER 4 • Accent fabrics Our window treatments were simple and chic. Panels of chenille brocade frame both sets of French doors and the arched window. Navajo-patterned pillows and a throw were added to the fireplace grouping, and pumpkin-colored pillows were scattered around the room for balance. Reproduction English rugs complete this layer.

LAYER 5 • Non-upholstered furniture (workhorses)
These workhorses of the room provide surfaces and storage. The homemade coffee table offers both. Two decorative iron pedestals, topped with a piece of glass, separates the club chairs. And with its lid closed, even the piano can serve as a buffet.

LAYER 6 • Accessories The accessories have been kept to a minimum, leaving breathing space for guests. Pictures, plates, bowls, and mementoes are kept fairly large in scale.

LAYER 7 • Plants & lighting A track light with a dimmer provides overall ambience, task lighting is available to each of the seating areas, and up lights create the drama.

Dining Room Drama

Intimacy is the main course

Our dining room was not so large, but it was very, very tall. Everything was about tall. This room's proportion problems didn't stop there. It had a huge, arched picture window on one wall, and a too-small window on an adjacent wall. On yet another wall was the entrance to a not-so-fabulous kitchen, without a door!

BEFORE

We wanted to achieve stature in this dining room and add old-world architectural embellishments that would look as if they had been part of the house since the day it was built. We wanted some drama, and also a place to display all of our wonderful accessories.

The arched picture window was the focal point of the room, so we naturally started there. Treating arched windows doesn't necessarily have to be a pain. My rule of thumb is that you can either use fabric or you can use shutters. I love the idea of shutters, but I still wanted an opportunity to bring fabric into the room. A dining room without fabric is a little cold, and if you're going to spend a long, romantic evening, romantic means fabric.

Custom-made shutters can be on the pricey side but are worth their weight in gold, especially on a window that serves as the centerpiece of the room. The circumference of the window was measured and a frame was built all the way around it to support the shutters. At the top of the window, a beautiful slatted arch was designed to match the shutters, allowing the shutters to move independently. This configuration gives us full control over the light entering the room. A few of the slats can be opened to let in sunlight or moonlight, or all of the slats can be opened to welcome in natural light. On the bottom section of the window we wanted the shutter slats to open vertically, making the room seem as tall as it really was and drawing the eye up to the fan light.

A huge arched window dominates the dining room, washing it with light but also leaving it stark and cold. My vision was to balance the window with a dramatic chandelier, and bring warmth into the room using rich, dark woods and saturated colors. Built-in shelving and an upholstered bench would create storage without intrusion.

Next we hung beautiful chenille brocade fabric panels from a pole that ran the entire width of the dining room above the window arch. The fabric drapes all the way down the wall on both sides of the window, where it falls in soft, luscious puddles on the floor. When the shutters are closed for privacy, there are still gorgeous fabric panels flanking each side of the window. When the shutters are open, they rest against the background of the fabric panels creating a continuous, uninterrupted view. *Fabulous!*

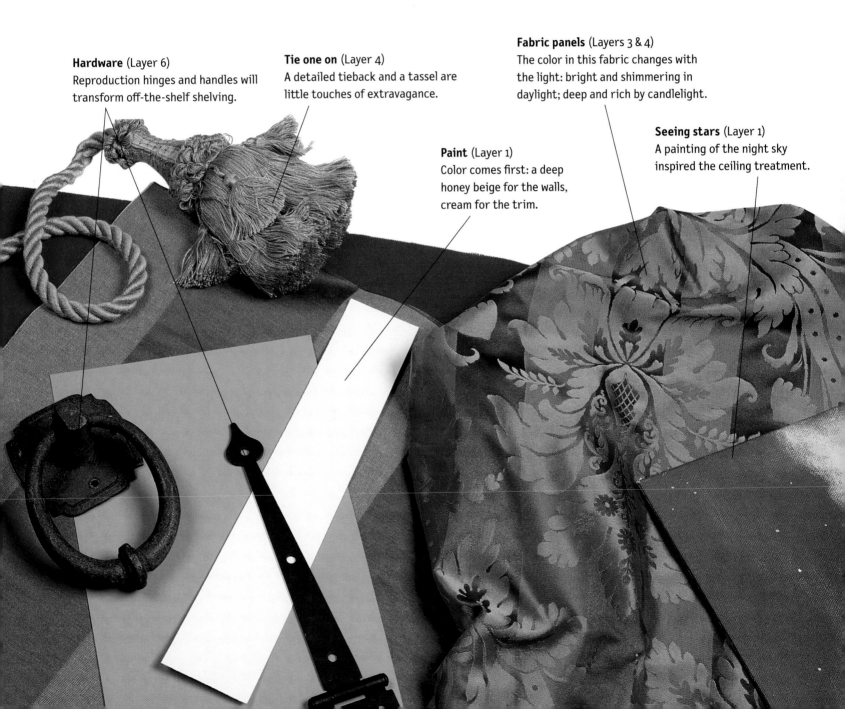

Hardware (Layer 6)
Reproduction hinges and handles will transform off-the-shelf shelving.

Tie one on (Layer 4)
A detailed tieback and a tassel are little touches of extravagance.

Fabric panels (Layers 3 & 4)
The color in this fabric changes with the light: bright and shimmering in daylight; deep and rich by candlelight.

Paint (Layer 1)
Color comes first: a deep honey beige for the walls, cream for the trim.

Seeing stars (Layer 1)
A painting of the night sky inspired the ceiling treatment.

HOME PLATE Our inspiration for this wonderful plate rack came from the idea of clutter-free living. We wanted to get as much clutter as possible out of the kitchen and up on the walls, where it would be eye-catching rather than in the way. Remember, there's power in grouping like objects. And we're going to put a whole lot of plates up on the wall.

Keep this in mind, though, when thinking about how to display your collections: too many individual plate racks could turn the wall into Swiss cheese, and we didn't want that. So we designed an entire wall surrounding the under-scale but fabulous window to maximize their impact by keeping them together. Got a good idea? Make it bigger!

We built two plate racks out of pine, each in the shape of a box and just deep enough to stand plates on the shelves. Once they were constructed, we took each box and bolted it to the wall. To play up this window a bit more, we took two pieces of plywood that were cut into an arch and sandwiched them together. Covering them with Flexall, our favorite plasterlike compound, we created an old-world look of textured plaster. The two plate racks were connected with a shelf that runs over the top of the window and is secured with L brackets. (For more detail, see pages 78–79.)

It's amazing what you can get through the mail these days. We ordered antique, hand-hewn barnwood beams from a catalog (see the Appendix) and ran them from wall to wall above each plate rack. Small blocks of the same old wood were placed

under the beams so that they appear to be supported on the wall. This connective element from the top to the bottom adds wonderful character to the space and makes it look as if it were part of the home's original wall.

Below the window we made a variation on a window bench with a couple of surprises. Out of simple plywood we built a long box and divided it into four cubbyholes, giving us great storage for decorative platters and china. And for the utilitarian but unattractive items, we added a row of piano-hinged cabinet fronts below the cubbyholes to hide the clutter. Love that!

To make the cabinetry look like it was crafted by a seasoned carpenter, we capped all the edges with half-round molding. Later we could add small lights the size of hockey pucks below the cabinet shelves to illuminate the space.

We used the same fabulous chenille brocade fabric to drape the window and tied it back with glorious, overscale tassels. On the window bench, we upholstered the back and seats in a stripe-on-stripe silk, then carried it down to a half-round padded cushion on the cabinet fronts below the seat. To bring the eye upward, we pleated the same stripe-on-stripe silk inside the arch over the window.

The areas on each side of the window are now identical and symmetrical. We placed all our beautiful display china in the plate racks, not only organizing them but adding a beautiful decorative statement to the wall. Very cool idea.

BEAM ME UP   Remember that other wall, which housed an entrance to the kitchen but had no door? We took our cue from the plate rack and created an illusion of two built-in hutches, even though—surprise—one of the hutches was really the entrance to the kitchen. Again, to match what we had done to the rest of the dining room, we needed to give this wall an architectural feeling that would be grand, would have balance, and would contribute some drama. I've said it a million times—when you can't build out, build up.

We started by adding four plywood columns across the wall, simple four-sided boxes attached to the wall and covered with our dear friend Flexall. Then we added another mail-order beam across the top and above the doors, uniting the columns into one modular unit. The doors to the hutch and kitchen were made from plywood covered with bead board and trimmed in pine. After faux finishing, they matched the beams perfectly. Great hinges of heavy iron hardware kept the old Spanish influence. Another beam was added between the center columns to act as our sideboard. All of this architectural embellishment takes up only ten inches of space from the wall! How fabulous is that?

The ledge in the center created a mantel feeling. It was dressed with a beautiful gold-leafed, round mirror that reflects the entire dining room. And above, we have room for more of our tchotchkes, but kept it simple, placing only one object in each cubbyhole. We backlit everything to give it a wonderful soft look.

> *'I've said it a million times—when you can't build out, build up.'*

We made these beadboard and pine doors ourselves and stained and distressed them to match the genuine antique beams. One set of doors leads to the kitchen, the other conceals a small storage area.

Plate rack

This attractive but inexpensive plate rack has the look of custom cabinetry. Like many of my fabulous fakes, it begins as just a simple plywood box. (You can also make the box out of pine boards.) Best of all, this design can be lengthened or widened to fit your own space. In our dining room, I built two plate racks to frame the arched window, and linked them with a ledge/shelf (see page 74). By painting them the same color as the wall, they became architectural embellishments as well as practical storage and display space.

what you'll need . . .

⅝-inch plywood	Finishing nails
¼-inch luan plywood	Hammer
Wood dowels, ¼-inch diameter	Miter box and saw, or coping saw
Power saw	Wood filler
Drill	Sandpaper
Wood glue	

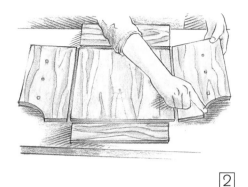 2

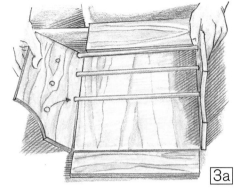 3a

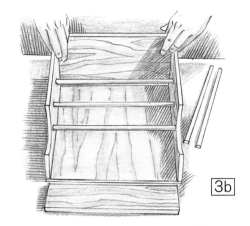 3b

1 This plate rack is basically a wooden box with a thin plywood back. Determine the dimensions of the plate rack by measuring both the size of your plates and the space on the wall. If the plate rack will be placed next to a window, match the height of the window. Space the shelves evenly, and an inch or two higher than the plates.

2 Cut out the sides, top, bottom, and shelves from ⅝-inch plywood. On each side, cut a decorative quarter circle at the bottom. Cut three wood dowels slightly longer than the inside width of the rack. Predrill holes for the wood dowels that will hold the plates in place on the shelves. Drill only halfway through the plywood.

3 Start with one side of the plate rack. Glue the dowels in place, then attach the shelves using wood glue and finishing nails driven from the outside. Attach the other side in the same way. Then glue and nail the top and bottom to complete the box, making sure the corners are square. Turn the box over and attach the back using a thin bead of glue and several small finishing nails.

4 Finish the front edges of the rack and shelves with half-round molding secured with small finishing nails. Attach the side molding first, then miter the other pieces to fit snugly. Fill any gaps or nail holes with wood filler, then sand and paint the same color as the walls.

 4

TABLE TALK   Next we replaced what I would describe as dorm furniture with something a little more adult. Since we typically spend several hours lounging at the dining room table, comfortable yet stylish chairs were a must. We were able to splurge on timeless leather chairs by skimping elsewhere, like building our own dining room table. We opted to seat six comfortably in a rectangle so that the guests can all look across to each other. The base is a reproduction that was purchased via mail order, and the tabletop is simply planks of pine that we distressed, then stained with bronzing powder. It was dramatically transformed into a burnished oak antique within a matter of days. It's a convincing impostor, and at a quarter of the price. Love that!

In the center of the room we created a beautiful hand-painted night sky on the ceiling as a backdrop to a dramatic Mexican chandelier. Flowers from our centerpiece reach right up to the chandelier.

The arrangement is elevated so that guests can see each other without having to peer around it. The flicker of candlelight and the soft light from the dimmed chandelier complement each other.

A large floral arrangement introduces a bright bouquet of hues for daytime, while appropriately placed candles will subtly boost the romantic ambience at night. Hanging a dramatic chandelier with small lampshades gave the room the warmth and coziness it deserves. Can you just imagine the light flickering on the paint and fabric in this room? Fabulous.

Remember to start your own dining room makeover with a sketch, and proceed layer by layer. Gather magazine and catalog clippings, paint chips, and fabric swatches and let them inspire you. Be creative and unafraid (I know you can do it!), and most important, just have fun. The dining room is a place for sharing special moments with friends. Now flip the page with me and I'll show you how we transformed our "before" photo into a beautifully finished room.

OPPOSITE: New shades transform the existing chandelier. By saving money elsewhere in the room, we were able to afford rich leather dining chairs.

ABOVE: Mirrors are fabulous room stretchers. They double the stuff you love while pulling light from a window to the other side of the room.

What was stark is now stylish. Love that!

LAYER 1 • Paint & architecture The huge arched window washed the room in natural light but left it stark and cold. We used rich, saturated colors to warm it up. The antique beams, discovered in a mail-order catalog, add both visual interest and storage space.

LAYER 2 • Installed flooring When it ain't broke, don't fix it! The solid oak flooring simply needed refinishing and an Oriental area rug added in Layer Four.

LAYER 3 • Upholstered furniture We took some of the money we saved elsewhere in the room and splurged on leather-upholstered dining chairs. But rather than use only one color, the eight chairs are done in complementary shades. The antique table is a convincing impostor we made ourselves.

LAYER 4 • Accent fabrics Drapes frame both the large arched window and the doorway to the dining room, allowing us to fine-tune the mood of the room from sun-washed to warm and intimate.

LAYER 5 • Non-upholstered furniture (workhorses) Built-ins take the place of side pieces in this smallish room, including antique-beam shelving and an upholstered bench opposite the mirror.

LAYER 6 • Accessories The dramatic mantelpiece mirror doubles the room and pulls the light and view to that side of the room.

LAYER 7 • Plants & lighting The chandelier has been customized with small lampshades painted to fit the room. Candles provide atmosphere, and cut flowers add color.

Even the Kitchen Sink

Fresh start for a tired kitchen

BEFORE

What we loved about this kitchen was that it was very airy and full of light. But the appliances needed replacing, the cabinets were made of a low-grade wood that didn't look so hot, there were lots of odd surfaces, the room lacked a focal point, and on and on.

We entertained the idea of ripping out the cabinets, the floor, and the appliances. But then we thought about the contractors who sometimes start the job, get halfway finished, and disappear. Could we live with the kitchen completely disrupted for months?

We were falling into a familiar trap of concentrating on everything we hate about a room and becoming stuck. But by employing the art of disguise and the philosophy that you "add to" rather than "rip out," you can save yourself a lot of money and still have a wonderful room.

At one end of the kitchen was a laundry room. It had a sink along the same wall as the kitchen sink, with a back-door entryway in between. That made the laundry area and kitchen one big space. We started our makeover by creating a wall of shelves only six inches deep between the kitchen counter and back door, up to the ceiling and across to a bank of cabinets on the opposite wall. Frosted glass along the whole back of the shelf area provided a backdrop for colorful glasses and bowls. With the shelves we divided the space with a nice pass-through while retaining the natural light and adding height to the end of the room. With the diffused light shining through the frosted glass, those oil and vinegar bottles never looked so good!

We followed the same line of shelves from the divider along the wall above the kitchen sink and installed shelves to the end of this counter, too. Simple pine was trimmed with half-round molding and supported with L brackets. The shelves, which continued all the way to the end of the room, were painted in a gray accent

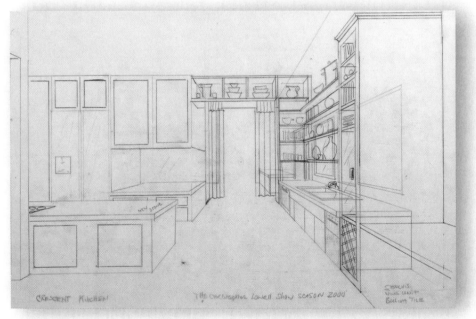

Portrait of a tired kitchen: old wood cabinets, outdated appliances, scuffed-up floor. Since we couldn't afford the headache of a major remodel, we added to rather than ripped out. The plan was to "disappear" the laundry room, then add surfaces and storage areas along the entire wall. Watch what happens ...

color. When combined with the frosted architectural glass, the shelves added a very high-tech element to the room. It looks sensational.

Beyond the counter beside the kitchen sink, we decided to add a tall custom cabinet that would create a bridge between the kitchen counter area and the breakfast nook. By not replacing all the cabinets, we were able to afford this great wine-cookbook-storage-phone station thingy. We kept the cost down here, too, by using simple, paint-grade pine lumber instead of a really expensive wood. When it arrived, I watched as the deep crown molding was put into place on top of the built-in. It's the crown molding that says "rich"—had to have it!

The balancing act in this room was between warm, somewhat neutral materials and cool, high-tech touches. I love the glitter and practicality of stainless steel in a kitchen, and it played a wonderful supporting role in this room.

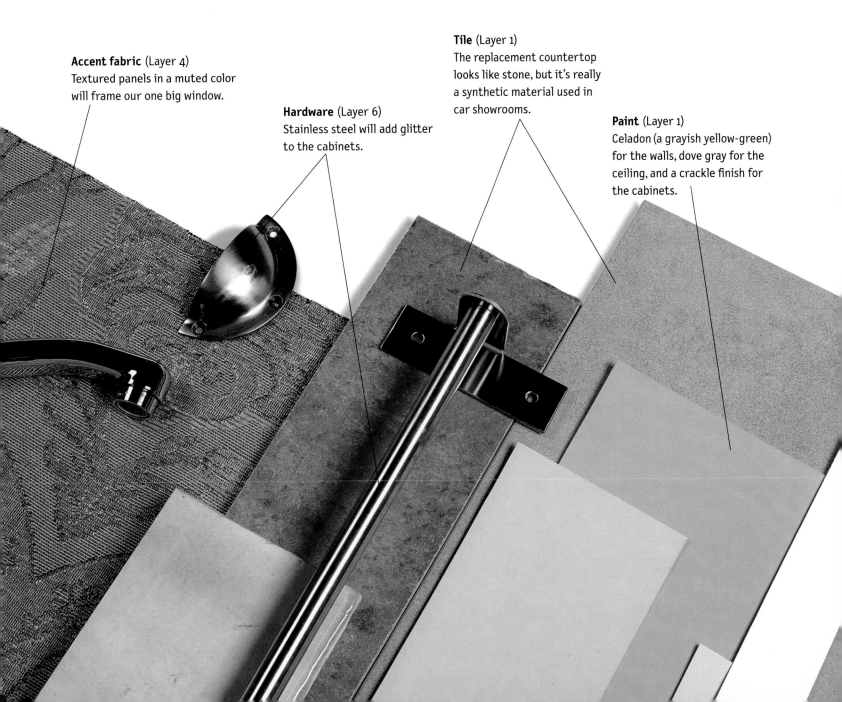

Accent fabric (Layer 4)
Textured panels in a muted color will frame our one big window.

Hardware (Layer 6)
Stainless steel will add glitter to the cabinets.

Tile (Layer 1)
The replacement countertop looks like stone, but it's really a synthetic material used in car showrooms.

Paint (Layer 1)
Celadon (a grayish yellow-green) for the walls, dove gray for the ceiling, and a crackle finish for the cabinets.

Shelving and cabinetry tie together the kitchen and breakfast nook. But it's not custom—it's plywood! The upper shelves are supported with L brackets, and the cubbyholes are simple plywood boxes designed to fit twenty-four store-bought baskets.

ADVENTURES IN SPACE   At the entryway to the kitchen we created a wonderful cabinet that has almost a library feeling and yet remains kitchen-practical. Near the top, the cabinet has cubbyholes for glasses of all shapes and sizes. Just below is an area for a stash of wine bottles. Farther down is a letter area for holding all of those unpaid bills. The desk area underneath is large enough to hold a portable phone or a stack of cookbooks. Along the side of the cabinet are small storage drawers; they are great for keeping clutter—a stapler, coupons, pens, and all sorts of things cleverly concealed.

Down below we have a great little cooler for our white wine. If someone knocks on the door at the last minute, you can take one bottle out of the cooler and replace it with a bottle from the storage racks above. You've always got chilled wine—what a great host!

Deciding what to do with the cabinet fronts and countertops was a challenge. Initially we looked into replacing the cabinet fronts to see if it would be as inexpensive as they say it is. Although the cost of having them replaced was reasonable, it was still more money than our budget would allow. And we always say, "Faux finish, faux finish, faux finish." So we invited a friend to come in and create a painted crackle effect on all the cabinets in a fabulous celadon color. It added much-needed charm to the old wood we inherited, and helped keep us within our budget. Just because it's wood doesn't mean it's good. Don't be afraid to paint!

BE STEEL MY HEART We still needed to integrate a high-tech element into the cabinets. The room already had one accent: the stainless steel in some of the appliances. Remembering our goal of "adding to," we found fabulous stainless-steel

Pretty impressive! The wine cabinet holds not just wine (red above, white below) but also glasses, cookbooks, bills, even miscellaneous kitchen junk. The dramatic crown molding adds to the custom look.

87

ABOVE LEFT: It looks like stone, but this countertop is really a synthetic material used in car showrooms.

ABOVE RIGHT: Ceramic tile is a practical and less expensive alternative to authentic terra cotta.

OPPOSITE: A crackle finish lends a sophisticated look to those once-tired cabinets. The sleek stainless-steel handles are actually towel bars hung vertically. Faux-stone countertops and a few "picture-frame" tiles complete the look.

towel bars. Even though they're meant to be hung horizontally, we attached them vertically to the cabinets for door pulls. Now our cabinets have an old-world look with a hip new attitude. We also replaced the fronts of the other appliances with a do-it-yourself stainless steel kit (see the Appendix) and added a new faucet. Suddenly the sparkle of the stainless steel brings the eye all the way around the room and looks absolutely spectacular. And we saved so much money.

Since we chipped away at the budget, we were able to afford a new floor, new countertops, and some decorative tile work along the backsplash. Although the old floor was a neutral, solid, organic color, we felt that a new floor would give the kitchen some warmth. The terra-cotta-looking tiles anchor the room and add a warm contrast to the sparkle of the steel.

We replaced the old countertops with a synthetic material that is used in Europe as flooring in car showrooms. It looked great and it was just the right thickness. All we had to do was remove the wood trim, drop in the new countertop, grout it, and put the trim back in place. We saved a ton of time and mess by covering up rather than replacing.

Behind the stovetop, over the sink, and under the freestanding cabinets we

Crackle-finish cabinets

Totally ripping out the kitchen in the house and starting from scratch simply wasn't in the budget. And just because the cabinets were wood didn't mean they were good. So instead of living with them—or using them for firewood—we decided to practice what we preach. We gave them a fabulous crackle finish that really saved the day and a whole lot of money. But choose colors carefully. Remember that the top coat color will be the primary color, with the base coat showing through the cracks.

what you'll need . . .

Fine-grit sandpaper	Glaze (gold and dark brown)
Masking tape	Paintbrushes
Water-based primer	Natural sea sponges
Base color latex paint (cream)	Disposable foam plates
Top color latex paint (celadon)	Polyurethane finish (semigloss)
Crackle medium	Rubber gloves

2a

2b

3

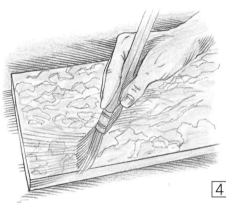

4

2 Moisten a sea sponge with water, dip it in the top color and dab the color over the crackle medium. Use a generous amount of paint and do not go back over the paint that has been applied. The crackling will begin within three to five minutes. Work quickly for consistency. Let dry. As a variation, you can get a streaked effect by applying paint in one direction with a brush.

3 Dip a moistened sea sponge in the gold glaze and rub in a circular motion over the crackled finish. Repeat with the dark brown glaze. It's not necessary to let the first glaze dry before applying the second glaze.

4 When the doors are completely dry, seal them with clear polyurethane in a semigloss to protect the crackle finish. When this final coat is dry, reinstall the hinges and rehang the doors. For these cabinets we created handles from towel bars!

1 The job is easier if you remove the cabinet doors and hardware, and work on a flat surface. Lightly sand the door fronts and wipe them clean. Mask any areas you don't want to paint, then apply a coat of primer. Let dry, then apply the base color. When the base color is dry, brush on the crackle medium and allow this to dry according to the manufacturer's directions.

added lovely celadon tiles to the backsplash. Some of the tiles were inset with small picture frames that added to the high-tech effect. We made sure to place tile where it would really stand out. This added to the illusion of having an abundance of tiles when in fact they were simply strategically placed. Guess what? We saved money again with this technique.

COFFEE KLATCH   The other end of the kitchen had a wonderful eat-in nook. Although the dining room is right around the corner, having a spot to gather for coffee is a wonderful feature. We found a very sleek stainless-steel table from a restaurant supply shop at bar height that was perfect. The table, which is only two feet wide and five feet long, has a shelf below for showing off all the serious cooking stuff that convinces your guests that you're a culinary whiz.

We placed 1950s diner stools around the table and now have a place to eat in the kitchen. The table also doubles as a place to garnish the plates just before you serve your guests in the dining room. Above the table we hung some gourmet utensils and great big glass globe lights. They're large in scale and work well here.

We wanted to play up the view from the charming arched window at the end of the breakfast nook. To bring attention to the window we painted the walls a warm celadon color, trimmed the window with a cream color, and put a pole across the entire wall just above the arch. On each side of the window we hung straight fabric panels that can be closed for privacy. When opened, the panels are completely free of the great molding and sweet view. The fabric also changed the acoustics of this end of the room, where terra-cotta tiles and steel can create a hollow sound. This simple window treatment was all we needed to bring the window to life and add a rich warmth to the room.

The wall that contains the kitchen sink and counter continues into the breakfast nook area, where someone built a window bench. Usually I love window benches, but this was a real space robber. I also wanted to increase the storage area with cabinets that would be much more valuable in this kitchen than a bench.

We found some wonderful square wicker storage baskets and measured for shelves that would fit about twenty-four of them. We built a unit out of three-quarter-inch plywood with partitions for the baskets to slide in and out. We used half-round molding one more time to finish the edges. After it was painted and caulked, it looked like custom carpentry. The unit is three shelves high and four cubbyholes wide. Each cubbyhole holds two wicker baskets.

Can you imagine how wonderful this storage space is for entertaining? One basket holds all the napkin rings. Another one has the napkins, another the silver you don't use all the time. What a fabulous way to keep clutter out of sight while saving the kitchen cabinets for utilitarian utensils and pantry items—the stuff you use every day.

Above the shelf unit, we continued the same shelves we

'*Just because it's wood doesn't mean it's good! Don't be afraid to paint— it opens up so many options.*'

We've created a place for every possible kitchen utensil, glass, plate, and gadget you can imagine. The nicer things can be displayed on open shelves *(below)*; kitchen junk and lesser-used items can be stored out of sight in baskets *(right)*.

used over the kitchen counter all the way to the end of the room. Here we filled the shelves with bowls, plates, frosted glasses and all those wonderful serving pieces that are usually hidden inside the cabinets.

For lighting, we added an inexpensive high-tech cable system over the food-prep area. This gave us a chance to spotlight work areas without destroying the ambience. We added two drop lights over the nook table and put them on a dimmer so that guests would feel comfortable. No matter how hard you try to shoo them elsewhere, guests love to congregate in the kitchen, so we wanted the mood to be inviting.

One of the reasons we wanted to redo this kitchen was to find great space-saving ways to avoid clutter and display our decorative pieces. We kept in mind our principle of "adding to" versus "ripping out." We saved money because we were flexible and employed the art of disguise. And we have a fabulous, functional kitchen. *Love that!*

You may never get guests out of the kitchen once they belly up to the breakfast bar. The stainless-steel utility table also serves as a kitchen-prep surface and as a staging area for the adjacent dining room. Natural light floods the kitchen during brunch; the fabric panels can be drawn for an intimate wine tasting.

High tech meets old world. Now you're cooking!

LAYER 1 • Paint & architecture Shelves running the entire length of the kitchen separate spaces and make for a great functional window treatment. Celadon—a grayish yellow-green—was the color for our walls and architectural tiles, while the ceiling was done in a dove gray to match the shelving. The cabinets were then faux-finished in a celadon over cream crackle finish.

LAYER 2 • Installed flooring By saving money elsewhere we splurged on a tile floor. It's low-maintenance and doesn't show dirt.

LAYER 3 • Upholstered furniture For a cool, retro look we added four black stools to the "coffee klatch" area of the kitchen. Since we were balancing high tech against old world, we kept major upholstery to a minimum.

LAYER 4 • Accent fabrics Here again, fabric was kept to a minimum to keep the food-prep areas free and functional. The window at the end of the room was enhanced by a cheap closet dowel with floor-to-ceiling panels flanking both sides.

LAYER 5 • Non-upholstered furniture (workhorses) A wine rack/storage unit, stainless-steel table with shelf below, and resurfaced countertops are the workhorses of this room.

LAYER 6 • Accessories Every inch of the space has been decorated with dining and cooking stuff in order to free up cupboards for pantry items. One of the great accents in the room is stainless steel—by resurfacing the existing appliance fronts we were able to further play up the drama.

LAYER 7 • Plants & lighting All that was needed were a few dried wreaths and colorful bowls of fruit to add a living element to the interior, especially since every window revealed nothing but lush flowers and green box hedges. Task lighting brightens the work areas without destroying the ambience.

Master Bedroom

Tropical punch for a boring bedroom

BEFORE

The master bedroom should be thought of as a ceremonial space in which you relax at the end of the day, drift off to sleep, and recharge yourself. Your most important goal with the master bedroom is to create a place of tranquillity where you feel utterly calm and serene. That was the principle guiding the makeover of this master bedroom, which went from an average room to a restful retreat with useful and enchanting spaces.

This master bedroom is typical of what many of you probably have in your homes. Rectangular in shape, with doors to a hall, bathroom, and patio, it had sufficient space. But I knew that with a little creativity and costuming it could be spectacular. In addition to the bed, I also envisioned a sitting area, plenty of storage and display space, even a place for meals and a work surface. But with these wonderful ideas, we still didn't want to forget our guiding principle. After all was said and done, it would still be a ceremonial space. With this in mind, we started with color (Layer One) and began creating our tranquil environment.

One of the things I love about sanctuary living is choosing colors that are both vibrant and mood-defining. Color gave this master bedroom its incredible karma. The primary background color used for the walls was a deep plum, while on the ceiling we used a soft violet. With a bamboo theme to come, we chose a deep mustard gold as our trim color. The combination of the two shades created a fabulous iridescent quality. If this sounds a touch Moroccan, a touch Balinese, well, that's what it's all about! The colors envelop you, and you no longer have a sense of the room's size or shape—just its mood.

ORGANIC INSPIRATION The inspiration for this master bedroom was a wonderful four-poster bamboo bed. Its bamboo canopy gave it an organic feeling that I really loved. When I think of sanctuary living, I think about honoring nature and the outdoors. I loved the versatility of the bamboo and looked for ways to incorporate it elsewhere in the room.

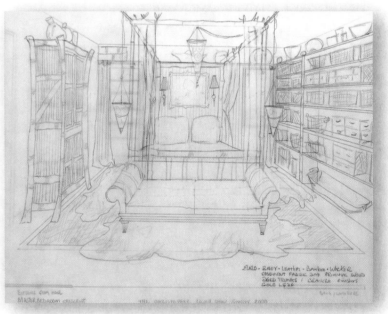

This master bedroom had sufficient space, but the doors and windows needed balancing. I loved the bamboo bed and decided to use that influence throughout the room. Shelving would be built out of plywood and then dressed with bamboo trim from a mail-order catalog; a Balinese armoire with a flare top would add a touch of whimsy.

Standing alone against one of the bedroom walls, the bed looked sort of *Gilligan's Island*-ish. Centered on the one wall without doors or windows, the bed was in the right place, but it definitely needed some company. So we built double bookcases from three-quarter-inch plywood on each side of the bed. On the front of the bookcases we widened the edges using plywood strips. When painted, they would look like custom cabinetry.

The paint and architecture details of Layer One create the serene mood of this bedroom, along with bamboo and other exotic materials used in unexpected places. Fabric serves as a connecting device, relating the bed to the windows to a backless settee.

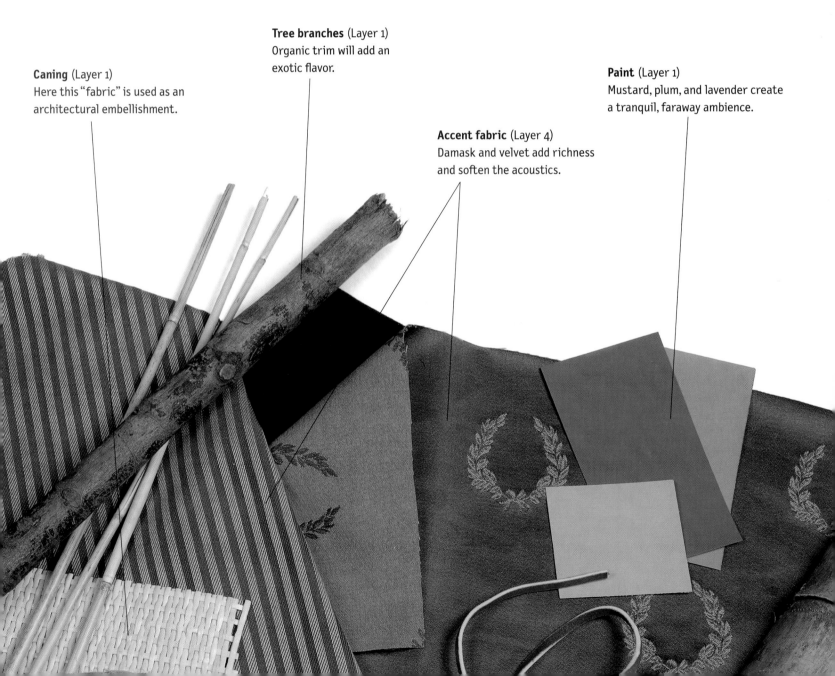

Caning (Layer 1)
Here this "fabric" is used as an architectural embellishment.

Tree branches (Layer 1)
Organic trim will add an exotic flavor.

Accent fabric (Layer 4)
Damask and velvet add richness and soften the acoustics.

Paint (Layer 1)
Mustard, plum, and lavender create a tranquil, faraway ambience.

ABOVE: The bamboo bed needed anchoring on the wall, so we built double bookcases from three-quarter-inch plywood on either side. The next step was to widen the horizontal and vertical edges of the bookcases with wood strips before attaching bamboo trim.

OPPOSITE: Bamboo columns from a mail-order catalog were split and attached to the bookcases. The deep plum wall color and rich mustard trim look great against the bamboo, helping to set the wonderful mood of this bedroom.

We found fabulous split-bamboo columns from a mail-order catalog and added them to the front of the bookcases. The bamboo pieces were about six feet long and four inches in diameter. We attached the half-round pieces to all of the vertical and horizontal rails on the face of the bookcases. So easy!

If you don't feel inclined to build the bookcases yourself, purchase inexpensive, assemble-it-yourself bookcases from a home center. Join the bookcases side by side along the wall, and add a wide strip of wood to the vertical and horizontal edges, accommodating the split bamboo pieces. Bolt the entire structure to the wall, and you have a terrific area for storage and display. Easier!

With the bookcases surrounding it, the bed looks built-in and anchored on the wall. The bed has a home, it's encircled by its bookcase friends—everyone's happy. The bookcases are only a foot in depth, but imagine how much storage you can get in just one foot. When you can't build out, build up.

BALI HIGH The bamboo influence was also carried throughout the room by applying more split bamboo pieces to the bathroom and bedroom doors. We attached vertical half-rounds of the bamboo around the perimeter of the doors, and then created a divider using a horizontal bamboo piece, slightly above the midpoint of the door. We then glued caning material bought from a catalog inside the bamboo frame, and stained it to soften the tone. Finally, we added wonderful cording around the bamboo and door handles. Very cool and right in keeping with our faraway theme.

The previous owners had recessed an entertainment center into the wall opposite the bed. It was slightly under-scale and didn't match our theme very well. We thought about plastering it over to match the rest of the room, but the cost would have been prohibitive. So here again the art of disguise came into play.

Adding doors to a recessed entertainment center provided dual function in this room. When closed, the doors hide unattractive equipment; when open, they add a shutter-like effect to the room. Dressed with bamboo and a caning fabric, they fit right into our South Seas environment.

We added doors to the entertainment center and covered them with the same caning material that we used for the bedroom doors. We trimmed the caning with bamboo, creating wonderful raised panels. The doors were then attached to the wall with swing hinges. When they're open, they create a dramatic shutter effect on the wall. Isn't that cool? We used what we already had and just dressed it up to match our theme.

The wall adjacent to the bed was tricky. At one end was a very short window, and at the other end a long door leading to the patio. To balance them on the wall, they needed to look the same size. To achieve this, we used plantation-style venetian blinds that extended from floor to ceiling at the window. This is one of my fabulous "chic cheats" that I use to bring symmetry to a space that would otherwise look unbalanced. These two long columns of blinds, in a wonderful wood and bamboo color, were flanked on both sides by fabric panels in a rich, deep plum. Now everything is uniform.

Between the door and the window we added a gorgeous Balinese armoire. What we loved about this piece was that it was overscale and organic, like the bed. The fabulous flared top added a touch of whimsy to the room. We continued the look all the way up to the ceiling by placing an antique toolbox—a flea-market find—on the top.

THE LITTLE SETTEE THAT COULD   I didn't want to ignore the area at the foot of the bed. It's a pass-through space leading to a hall at one end and a patio door at the other. It might seem an unlikely area to furnish, but you know me—I love upholstery in a room. This was a place where we could incorporate some fabric and also get some mileage out of an unused space.

We found a wonderful backless settee and placed it at the foot of the bed. We piled this little jewel, covered in a luxurious brocade fabric, with fluffy throw pillows. Having an upholstered piece here helps bring the focal point to the bed and elongates its presence in the room. We also added a small wicker table in front of the settee, where you can rest a cup of tea. Now this space serves a dual function. It's a fabulous place to sit in repose, read a good book, watch a little television, or enjoy a beverage. Love that!

As you look around the room, notice that we used fabric as a connecting device. Starting with the wonderful fabric panels hanging from the bed canopy, we also draped the wall behind the headboard with the same fabric. On the bed cover we used a rich plum twill with a wheat pattern. We used the same fabric in reverse colors on the bed skirt. The solid plum fabric on the window bridges the brocades in the upholstery with the bed linens.

Introducing another textured fabric into this room also worked with our sanctuary theme. In this case, it's a fake fur from a home furniture store, which we placed on the floor. We scattered white faux-fur rugs all the way around the room on top of a grass mat. This gave the room a well-traveled European look. Anytime you feel like you're on vacation at home, you've succeeded in creating a special environment. Congratulations!

When we have large areas like the bookcases to merchandise, I like to find one object that works anywhere in the room. For this room, we ordered decorative wooden boxes and stacked them on the shelves of the bookcases. We also placed them on the opposite side of the room in the entertainment center. It's a great way to connect everything together. Plus, they're great organizers for personal items that don't need to be displayed.

But my favorite item in the entire room was the full-length bamboo bed table. We made a simple top from stained pine and covered it with the same caning fabric used throughout the room. The legs are made from PVC pipe, of all things! But we cleverly stained and painted them with oil-based paint to simulate bamboo. By attaching casters to the legs, we created a table that can be wheeled over the bed for working or eating, then whisked back for sleeping (see photo on page 107).

Every room should have at least one upholstered piece. Our bedroom settee is the perfect place for a morning cup of tea or for draping a dressing gown.

Jungle door

A plain, hollow-core door becomes a canvas for imagination in the master bedroom. We were inspired by the idea of bringing nature indoors through the use of caning fabric and half-round bamboo pieces. If your local craft or fabric store doesn't carry these materials, check our Appendix (page 166). This is an easy project that can be done in a weekend. We love that!

what you'll need . . .

Hollow-core door

Roll of caning, 24 inches wide

Scissors

Glue roller

All-purpose adhesive

Straight tree branches, 1½-inch diameter

Electric or hand saw

Drill

2½-inch wood screws

Split bamboo halves, 4-inch diameter

Universal tint, brown

Polyurethane finish (gloss)

Paintbrush

Rags

Braided nylon rope, ½-inch diameter

Glue gun

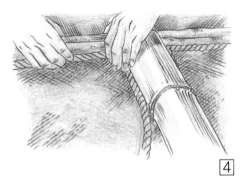

1 Using scissors, cut a piece of caning the length of the door. Using a glue roller or paintbrush, apply adhesive to the back of the caning. Wait thirty minutes until the glue is tacky. Adhere the caning to the door, smoothing out all air bubbles with a glue roller. Use adhesive in a well-ventilated area and wear a mask and gloves for protection.

2 Cut as many branches as needed for two rows around the perimeter of the door. Cut one piece of split bamboo to fit snugly across the door between the rows of branches. Cut notches in the inner rows of branches and miter the corners of the bamboo for a close fit. Predrill pilot holes in the branches and bamboo and then screw them to the door.

3 Add a bit of brown universal tint to a small container of polyurethane gloss finish. Apply the finish to the caning a little at a time with a paintbrush. Wipe it off immediately with a rag to produce an antiqued look. Repeat for deeper color.

4 Cut enough braided nylon rope to fit around the inside of the panels, then hot-glue it to the panel. The rope will help hide any gaps between the branches, bamboo, and caning. The ends of the rope can be carefully melted with a match or lighter to prevent fraying.

ABOVE: You can have a chic and cheap table by turning over an outdoor pot, draping it with fabric, and adding a rope tie and a glass top.

RIGHT: Every room needs at least one striking piece, and this Balinese armoire holds its own against the bamboo bed. Its flared top adds a bit of fun to our sanctuary space.

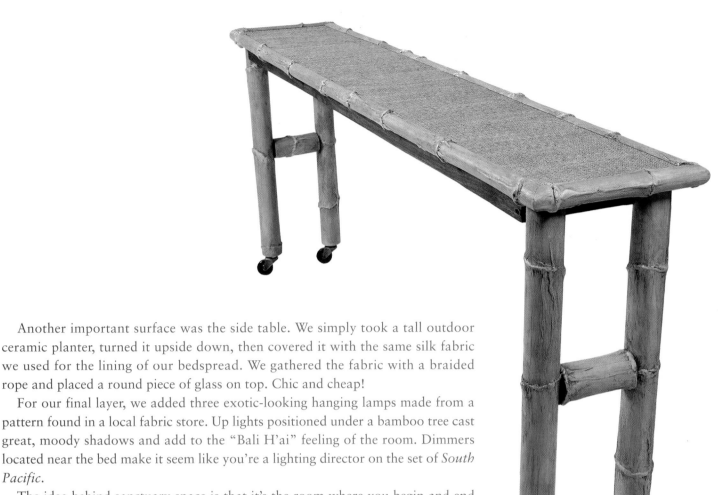

Another important surface was the side table. We simply took a tall outdoor ceramic planter, turned it upside down, then covered it with the same silk fabric we used for the lining of our bedspread. We gathered the fabric with a braided rope and placed a round piece of glass on top. Chic and cheap!

For our final layer, we added three exotic-looking hanging lamps made from a pattern found in a local fabric store. Up lights positioned under a bamboo tree cast great, moody shadows and add to the "Bali H'ai" feeling of the room. Dimmers located near the bed make it seem like you're a lighting director on the set of *South Pacific*.

The idea behind sanctuary space is that it's the room where you begin and end each day. It's your ceremonial spot and it needs to feel peaceful and tranquil. For those of you who just moved into a new house, get this room finished first. You'll have a peaceful place to unwind and relax.

By employing the art of disguise, having color courage, and being just plain inventive we have transformed our charmless bedroom into a cozy sanctuary. I may just make like Hugh Hefner and never leave the bedroom.

Great for a late-night snack or evening work, this bamboo-looking table glides over the bed with its PVC-pipe legs and casters. When it's time for sleep, just roll it down to the foot of the bed!

Create a place where you feel utterly calm and serene.

LAYER 1 • Paint & architecture Rich colors set the tone: deep plum, dusty lavender, and mustard. Bamboo and caning transform basic bookcases and doors into exotic pieces.

LAYER 2 • Installed flooring We simply cleaned up the inherited wood floor in preparation for Layer Four.

LAYER 3 • Upholstered furniture The bamboo four-poster bed inspired the whole Balinese theme. A backless settee extended the bed visually and provided yet another functional area.

LAYER 4 • Accent fabrics Keeping the bedcovers neutral allowed us to have fun with other fabrics. Velvet unites the door and window, and rich stripes frame the bed. Our floor is layered with sea grass and faux-fur skins for barefoot comfort.

LAYER 5 • Non-upholstered furniture (workhorses) A whimsical armoire and an African chest free up limited closet space. Our fabulous rolling table and chic cheat side table put everything at arm's reach.

LAYER 6 • Accessories Against this dramatic backdrop, inexpensive import items and flea-market finds become suddenly important.

LAYER 7 • Plants & lighting Down lights, up lights, and a cluster of hanging silk lamps illuminate our "well-traveled" South Seas look.

Bathroom Retreat

Dated? Dowdy? Do deco!

Is your bathroom driving you a little psycho? Did you inherit weird-colored tile, funky old fixtures, and one of those not-so-attractive clear shower curtains? What can you do? Well, the shower curtain is simple, but let's talk about the rest.

Often we don't have the luxury of designing a bathroom from scratch. You know me, I'm always trying to show you how to build on what you already have. If you can spruce things up by "adding to," you'll be able to bring the room into the new millennium much more quickly than if you were to wait until you could afford to level your bathroom and start from scratch. And who wants to be without a bathroom for three to four months? Not me!

In this bathroom, we inherited a plum-colored tile that we think is actually quite smart. When we saw the tile, rather than thinking "dated" we instantly thought "deco," which quickly became the motif for this bathroom. I've said it before and I'll say it again: If something about a room jumps out at you, use it to your advantage rather than dwelling on its age or seeming lack of style. You can make it hip with a little costuming.

One of the things we didn't like, however, was the contrast between the plum tiles and the white walls. If you have an odd or dated color (like this plum, or butter yellow, or that 1950s combination of pink and green), don't paint your walls white thinking that it will somehow play the colors down. Trust me, the only thing it will do is play that funky color up! Instead, using a deeper shade of the same color will make it look intentional, and that's the effect we want.

That's what we did here. We found a wonderful companion color paint that was a touch darker than the plum in our tile, and painted the walls with it. The transformation of the bathroom began with just that coat of paint.

Architecturally, we took a look at what we could build upon to increase the bathroom's function (remember, architectural embellishments are still a part of Layer One). In this bathroom there was a vanity cabinet beneath two frosted-glass

BEFORE

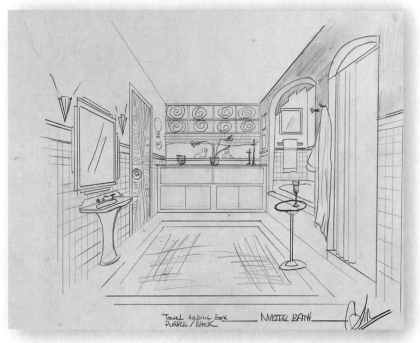

The inspiration for this older bathroom came from the plum-colored tiles we inherited. The color screamed deco, and that quickly became our theme. New fixtures, faux finishing, fabric, and black accent tiles would complete the look and give this bathroom a millennium lift.

windows. We wanted to add height to the room, so we built a great big box out of three-quarter-inch plywood, with six cubbyholes, and attached it to the wall above the windows. Now, not only does the bathroom have height, it also has an area for storage or display.

The cubbyholes were constructed in a grid design with half-round molding on all the horizontal and vertical edges. You've seen me do that a million times, and it saves so much finishing work. We painted the box and cubbyholes black to match the rest of the vanity.

The entire vanity area had been done in an inexpensive grade of honey-colored veneer plywood. We didn't like its appearance, and it certainly wasn't very deco.

Plum, black, and silver were the driving forces behind our deco bathroom. A darker shade of the plum on the tiles became the wall color, while black tile in the shower and tub provided a monochromatic, modern twist. Yes, fabric works in the bathroom!

Hardware (Layer 6)
Chrome and stainless fixtures are the glittering "jewelry" of this room.

Tile (Layer 1)
New black tile will complement the old plum.

Sushi towels (Layer 6)
Instead of hiding your towels, display them.

Fabric (Layer 4)
This stripe-on-stripe will be a valance over the bath area.

Paint (Layer 1)
A darker shade of plum for the walls, but lighter trim.

Doorknob (Layer 1)
An ornate finial will become a classy doorknob.

Diligent masking helps preserve what you already have during the painting process, in this case the 1930s tile. A plywood box, poised and ready to be mounted above the windows, will provide much-needed storage in this small room.

The drawers were sent out for faux finishing and came back in a sleek black finish. Inspired, we replicated the same finish on the cabinet doors. Now the entire wall ties together and matches the black trim tile in the rest of the room. And faux finishing was less expensive than completely resurfacing, so we saved money there. Cha-ching. I love that.

The top of the vanity had several budget-grade marble tiles that needed replacing. We took a piece of luan plywood, painted a lovely mottled faux finish on it, and covered the entire vanity top. It looks great.

The frosted-glass windows above the vanity didn't add much to the room. There was no view outside, and privacy wasn't an issue. We attached mirrors over the frosted glass so that we had a nice long vanity that doubled the visual size of the room. It was a better use of this space than the not-so-hot frosted-glass windows. It looks stunning.

The very plain doors leading into the bathroom had to be pretty stunning, too, so we faux-finished them in a fabulous grained treatment. First we took a window squeegee and cut notches out of the rubber strip. Then we painted the existing,

A deeper shade of the inherited plum tile made our bathroom color scheme look intentional. A little faux finishing, new fixtures, some stair-stepped fabric over the tub and we're in business!

hollow-core door with a thick brown glaze, and dragged the squeegee across the surface to simulate an exaggerated grain pattern. To make the effect even more dramatic we created four triangle patterns. It's very deco and very cool. Both sides of each door were done with the same drag technique. When everything dried, we added great big finials for doorknobs.

WATERWORKS   Fixtures are the jewelry of a room. Accessorizing with plumbing fixtures in a bathroom is a terrific thing. If you're not sure how to do it, think in terms of your own wardrobe. If you open up your jewelry box, you wouldn't put everything on or you'd look like a lounge singer from Las Vegas. You would put a little sparkle in your hair, something on your finger, and a little more sparkle at your wrist, like a watch or bracelet. Well, bathrooms are exactly the same.

In the shower area, we installed a beautiful surface-mounted shower with a great big sunflower pan head. While we were installing the shower head, we discovered significant damage behind the wall. The problem needed fixing, which meant retiling, but we couldn't easily match the plum tiles that we had inherited. We

ABOVE: Fixtures are the jewelry of a room and add sparkle as well as function. Black tile was used to complement the inherited plum tile, and European fixtures give the tub and shower a sophisticated look.

OPPOSITE: Wall sconces found at a flea market inspired the deco-looking mirror, which was easily constructed with our favorites, luan plywood and paint.

decided to use inexpensive, four-inch black tiles, matching the accent color in the room. The entire inside of the shower was resurfaced in the black tile, and it all looks very chic. Good tip!

BEAUTY AND THE BATH   Over in the bathtub area we installed a European handheld shower fixture. We discovered that we had the same problem in the tub area as we did in the shower area—damage behind the wall. And again, because we couldn't find the same plum tiles to replace those on the tub wall, we used the same black tiles that we used in the shower. Now that one wall is black, matches the shower and looks just fine. In fact, it's the black tile and white grout that give the deco feeling a bit of a lift.

We put in a new sink that had a stair-step accent at each corner. Again, very deco. The faucets have small porcelain tops with the words "Hot" and "Cold" written on them. This little added touch helped transport us back to the '30s.

Over the sink, we installed two very deco wall sconces we found at a flea market. Along with the plum tile, it was these wall sconces that inspired the whole deco bathroom look. Around the mirror we added stair-step trim made from two pieces of luan plywood in graduated sizes. We cut them in a stair-step pattern, then painted one piece black and one silver to match the accent colors of the room. We stacked and laminated them together, then attached them to each side of the mirror (see pages 116–117). Fabulous!

Fabric accents in the room were introduced by hanging a wonderful Roman shade from the plywood box over the vanity. Even though we replaced the frosted glass with mirrors and probably won't close the shade very often, it is a fabulous window treatment. Continuing around the room, we used more fabric on a valance above the tub area. We hung the fabric, a velvet with a stripe-on-stripe pattern, by placing a lathing strip through its upper hem, then attaching it to the wall with finish nails. This again reinforces the deco theme.

I love what we did with fabric above the vanity. We took a gray towel and a white towel, rolled them up together, and stuck them in each of the six cubbyholes. In California we call it a sushi roll. This becomes an extraordinary graphic element in the room, and it's practical, too. Need a towel? Just grab one.

On the surface of the vanity is a beautiful still life of accessories. We placed candlesticks to add height and mood, but more important, to pull the silver color from all the other areas of the room over to the back wall. We also liked the fact that this cluster is doubled thanks to the reflection in the mirror behind it.

This bathroom looks very expensive, but when you think about it, we employed the art of disguise and found companion colors that really worked. We put a little bit of sparkle around the room in the same way you use jewelry to add touches of sparkle to your wardrobe. Our vintage wall sconces and plum tile inspired us, and we love the '30s look. A few fluffy towels, some wonderful perfume bottles, and suddenly we're not going psycho anymore!

Deco mirror

When we went from dowdy to deco in our bathroom, one of the key architectural elements was a "stair-step" frame around the medicine cabinet that matched the tub valance. The simple surround gave some real style to an otherwise non-descript fixture. This treatment works best with the type of medicine cabinet that is recessed into the wall. The surround is built up in layers, then simply hot-glued to the wall.

what you'll need . . .

One 4 × 4-foot sheet
  of ¼-inch luan plywood

Kraft paper

Straightedge

Marker

Scissors

Jigsaw

Glue gun

Sandpaper

Finishing nails

Hammer

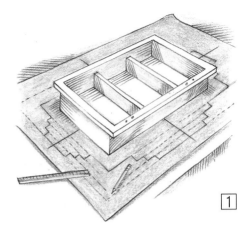

1

2

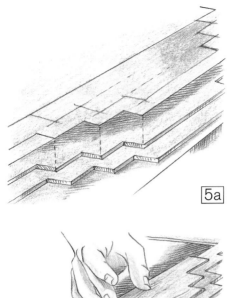

5a

5b

1 Remove the mirror from the medicine cabinet. Place the back of the cabinet on a piece of kraft paper and trace around it. Mark the center horizontal and vertical lines. Measure out from the cabinet outline in 1-inch increments all the way around. The overall width of the surround will depend on any other fixtures around the medicine cabinet, such as sconces, lights, switches, doors, or windows. Ours measured 4 inches wide.

2 Begin with the back layer, which will fit against the wall. Starting at the center point of each side, create a stair-step pattern, with each step 1 inch wide. The lengths can vary but must be equal distance from the center for symmetry. Cut the template from the paper, also cutting out the center for the cabinet.

3 Make a paper template for the second layer by following the first layer, but reduce the size of the steps by 1 inch. Cut out the template. The back and second layers will fully surround the medicine cabinet. Transfer the template to ¼-inch plywood and cut out both layers with a jigsaw. Sand the edges.

4 For the top layer, cut four individual pieces of luan, following the stair-step design of the previous layer. Reduce the size of the steps by 1 inch.

5 Paint or finish all pieces before assembling them. Hot-glue the layers together. Add a few small finishing nails to hold everything in place. Place the surround around the cabinet, and replace the mirror.

A deco look with a modern twist.

LAYER 1 • Paint & architecture We made a virtue of the existing plum-colored tile by creating an art deco look. Built-ins were spruced up with black laminate, hollow-core doors were faux-finished, and we added an open towel box to increase storage.

LAYER 2 • Installed flooring We loved the old floor with its black-tile band, and the white grout introduced a new color that we could play up in other layers, from towels to sink.

LAYER 3 • Upholstered furniture Rather than overcrowding this already-small bathroom, we placed a leopard-patterned ottoman around the corner in an adjoining dressing area.

LAYER 4 • Accent fabrics Instead of furniture, we used fabric to give the room an upholstered look. The plush rolled-up sushi towels and velvet tub valance help soften the architecture and fixtures.

LAYER 5 • Non-upholstered furniture (workhorses)
We couldn't resist the small chrome table, drawn up to the tub, to hold a glass of champagne during a long, relaxing soak.

LAYER 6 • Accessories Chrome fixtures are the jewelry of this bathroom. Silver is also spread around the room in the form of accessories such as candlesticks, a vase, and hardware.

LAYER 7 • Plants & lighting Flea-market wall sconces helped inspire the art deco theme. Placed on a dimmer, they can be used as either task or ambient lighting. Flickering candlelight and flowering plants relax the soul.

Home Office Haven

Costarring a clever desk and a hidden bed

For many of us, having a home office is a necessity, not a luxury. We conduct business out of our homes or have family computers, and we need a space for our office equipment. But where do we set up a home office? Unless you're fortunate enough to own a large home with a separate room to dedicate as an office, most of the time it's the guest bedroom that doubles as a work space. But you certainly don't feel professional sitting on a bed and working, laptop or not!

BEFORE

This small ten-by-twelve-foot room had an identity crisis. It didn't know if it was an office or a guest room. The truth is, it had to be both. Rooms that serve two functions, like this one, sometimes suffer from a decorating split personality. But with a touch of innovation and some space-saving smarts, this room could have both an identity and a generous dose of style.

What do home offices and guest bedrooms have in common? Organization! You need a place to hang clothes, a place to store office supplies, a desk for working, a bed for sleeping, and so on. By day, this room should look professional and be suitable for meeting clients and customers, even planning a corporate takeover or dot-com launch. By night, it should transform easily into a room that's comfortable and welcoming for overnight guests.

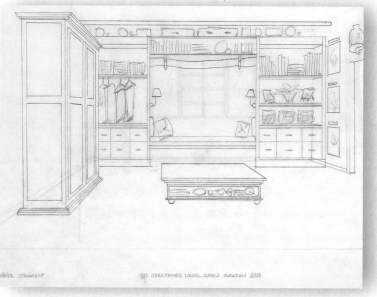

THE ART OF THE DESK   The first concept to keep in mind when planning your home office is that you need a surface where real work can be accomplished. Since work these days usually entails a computer for word processing or e-mail, it's essential to have a desk on which we can set up a computer workstation. But we also wanted to camouflage this desk during the evening when the room converts into a guest room. We didn't want to spend a fortune on a huge, expensive armoire that holds office equipment and then folds up to conceal everything. I figured that we could assemble something for a lot less money. And we did!

The key to this room was clever concealment. A Murphy bed, housed in an armoire, and a rollaway coffee table will increase the usable space, while built-in shelving around the window will provide ample storage for supplies. Fun containers will accessorize the room and serve a function, too.

We bought three inexpensive bookcases and a basic work table, out of which we would build a functional workstation. But remember, our space was only ten by twelve feet, so the configuration would have to be compact and yet still provide a work surface and some storage space.

Believe it or not, our inspiration was the library. Yes, the library! We arranged the bookcases perpendicular to the wall rather than flush against it. One bookcase was placed on the left side of the wall, far enough away from a closet so that the door could still open. The second bookcase was also placed perpendicular to the wall, on the right side, with the two bookcases' shelves facing each other. We left enough room between the bookcases to fit the work table. To create a continuous

Our paint and fabric choices reflect the duality of the room—professional, yet relaxed and comfortable. Molding spruces up built-in shelving and the armoire; textured fabric on a Roman shade adds depth without rivaling other fabric in the room. Cups, dowels, hanging rods, and finials will complete the room's metamorphosis.

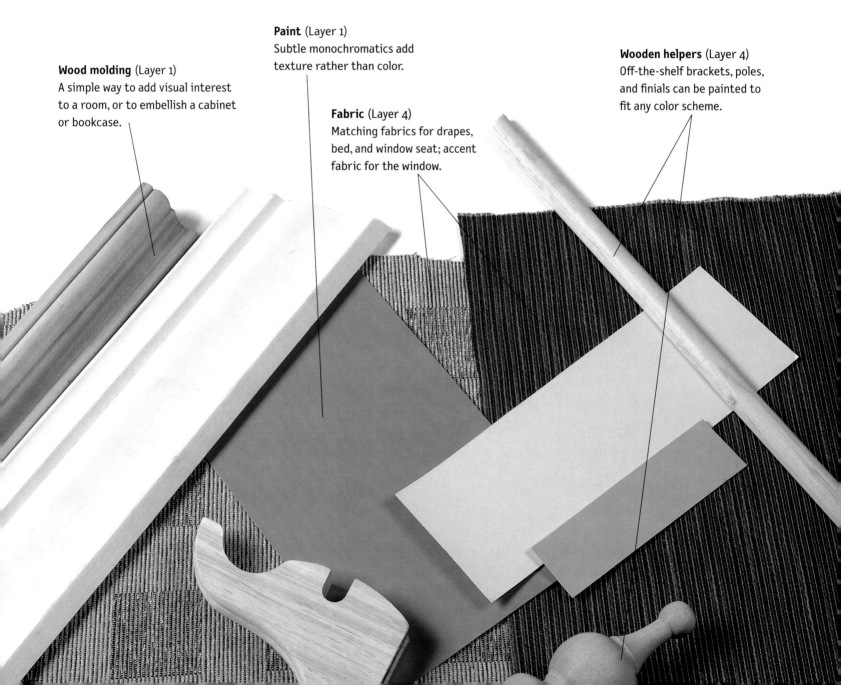

Paint (Layer 1)
Subtle monochromatics add texture rather than color.

Wood molding (Layer 1)
A simple way to add visual interest to a room, or to embellish a cabinet or bookcase.

Fabric (Layer 4)
Matching fabrics for drapes, bed, and window seat; accent fabric for the window.

Wooden helpers (Layer 4)
Off-the-shelf brackets, poles, and finials can be painted to fit any color scheme.

Sandwich a table between three bookcases (yes, three!) and you have an instant work surface. Two of the bookcases face the desk, while the third faces out, furnishing even more storage.

work surface, we adjusted the shelves on both of the bookcases to the same height as the table. Voilà! There's plenty of room for a computer monitor and keyboard, or a laptop, and even some space to spread out papers. If you have one of those massive computer-tower thingies, it will fit neatly under the table.

But we weren't finished yet with our fabulous workstation. We placed a third bookcase back-to-back with the bookcase on the right side of the table. We bolted the two bookcases together, and then to the wall. Now you have shelves facing the work table, and on the other side there are yet more shelves for storage or display. How cool is that?

Wooden brackets and a socket and dowel bridge the bookcases, creating an opportunity for more fabric and a smart solution for hiding the workstation. Pull the curtains and it's bye-bye desk!

The only problem was that we were left with a not-so-wonderful look where the two bookcases were joined back-to-back. Once dressed up, though, this area would look terrific. We simply took three mirrors and hung them from top to bottom along the sides of the joined bookcases. The mirrors pull the light and view from the window to the bookcases. On the single bookcase to the left of the desk, we hung a collection of inexpensive pictures that we selected from the art section of a superstore.

But there was still one thing left to do with the desk area. At night when this room would become a guest bedroom, we wanted the work area hidden. Who wants to see paperwork at night? Not me!

The solution was to install a pole and drapes between the two bookcases. When the curtains are open during the daytime, you work happily away at the desk. But at night, just draw the curtains closed and it all disappears. You're in business—or out of business—for the night. (A quick tip: use wooden rings for effortless opening and closing.)

STORAGE FOR TWO   This small room had a fabulous wall with an enormous window in the center. Although it framed a beautiful view of the green hedges outside, it cut into our usable wall space. So what did we do? We followed my own advice, "If you can't build out, build up."

We installed shelves and storage all the way around the window with standard three-quarter-inch plywood. Since this room was a guest bedroom at night, we

Rollaway table

In our home office the roll-away table does double duty in the conversion from home office to guest bedroom. It serves as a table for guests' morning coffee, or as a work surface for spreading out paperwork during the day. By varying the dimensions, this piece could be anything from a living room coffee table to a rollaway TV cart. Note that the table on the next page was done in reduced size for demo purposes.

what you'll need . . .

Measuring tape	Base molding and trim
One 4 × 8-foot sheet of ¾-inch plywood	Miter box and saw
Power saw	Hammer
Wood screws	Finishing nails
Screwdriver	Wood putty
Wood glue	Sandpaper
Four casters	¾-inch half-round molding
Trim molding	

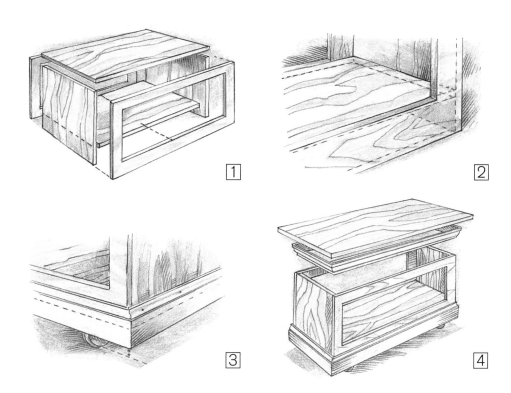

1 Determine the height, length, and width that you will need for the bench to fit under a window seat or stand alone as a coffee table. Be sure to leave enough room for the casters that will be attached to the bottom. From ¾-inch plywood, cut the front and back of the table as rectangles with the centers cut out—much like a picture frame. The dimensions of the frames will be determined by the width of the base molding. Cut solid sides for the bench from ¾-inch ply-wood. Assemble the box with glue and screws, recessing the sides between the front and back.

2 From ¾-inch plywood, cut the bottom shelf to the inner dimen-sions of the box and attach it level with the picture-frame cutout. This creates a ledge at the bottom. Attach casters to each of the four corners.

3 Cut the base molding to the appropriate dimensions, mitering the corners. Attach it to the bottom using finishing nails, leaving clearance for the casters to move freely.

4 Cut a piece of plywood for the top of the bench, leaving over-hang to accommodate the trim molding that will fit between the sides and top. Attach the top to the box using wood screws. Cut the top mold-ing to fit, mitering the corners. Attach the molding underneath the top with finishing nails. Fill all seams and screw holes with wood putty. Sand, prime with a stain-blocking primer, and paint.

Ta-da! The office is now a guest room once we draw our well-placed curtains and pull down the Murphy bed, wonderfully situated in a handsome armoire.

knew we needed a wardrobe for hanging clothes. We determined the depth by using a simple, ordinary clothes hanger. We just increased the width of the clothes hanger by a couple of inches on both sides, and that was the measurement for the entire built-in cabinet around the window.

On the left of the window we built an area for hanging clothes, and added shelves below. A cup-and-pole combination worked as our wardrobe rod, and we found sleek galvanized-tin storage bins that would fit on the shelves below. Now our guests will be comfortable, with a wardrobe for hanging clothes and nice bins for socks and undies.

We boxed in the window and added plywood shelves on the right-hand side of the wall, exactly the same size as our shelves on the left. I always try to find innovative opportunities for storage while still showing a flair for merchandising, and these lustrous modern bins really show off our style. Sticky notes, index cards, big markers all go in them. Without attractive containers to hold office supplies, it's clutter city.

Above the window there's a clean ledge for suitcase storage, decorative hatboxes, whatever you might need out of the way. To cut down on sanding and finishing the plywood, we put half-round molding over all the vertical and horizontal areas. It looks like fine cabinetry but costs much less. It's a wonderful trick.

Next we added a pole-and-drape combination across the wardrobe space on the left and the shelves on the right. Just as with the desk area, you can pull the drape to hide the wardrobe and shelves. Fabulous! We built a wonderful window seat as a connecting device between the two built-ins, and furnished it with an upholstered foam cushion for comfort. And there's one last little surprise in this room.

What if we want to sit on the window seat and enjoy a cup of coffee? There's no table for our drink. Oh yes there is—right under the window seat! We built a little coffee table and put it on casters so that during the daytime, it rolls right out and instantly there's a spot for your newspaper and coffee (see pages 126–127). It's also a great place for papers when we're hosting a meeting. Who'd have thought you'd get that in addition to everything else in this room? The wheels allow us to tuck it completely under the window seat when we're not using it. Don't you love it when things do double duty?

To transform the room from home office to guest bedroom, we simply remove the accessories from the top of the rollaway coffee table, place them on the table's lower shelf, and roll the table underneath the window seat. On the right, we pull the curtain across the shelves and no more office. On the left, we pull the curtain across the wardrobe and no more socks and undies.

MURPHY'S LAW So where's the bed? That's the coolest thing of all. It lives in a wonderful armoire that we had built by a fabulous carpenter. Guess what's coming back, folks? The Murphy bed. The bed mechanism bolts to the floor, rather than the wall. The stress is all on the floor, and there are no worries about finding studs in the wall. It's spring-loaded, with an easy-to-deploy, fold-down foot. We simply open the armoire, lower the bed, and our guests are set for the night.

To make the sleeping spot even cozier, we wired three lights the size of hockey pucks inside the top of the armoire. We added a touch switch near the bed that controls the brightness level. When our guest is in bed, he or she can conveniently bring the light up for reading, or down for relaxing. Now that's plush!

And the final touch? We fluffed up the window seat with some coordinating throw pillows that match an upholstered chair in the room. When preparing for your guest, pull a couple of pillows off the window seat and place them on the bed. It all ties neatly together.

Put the corporate takeover on hold—you're ready for company!

'Guess what's coming back? Ta-da—the Murphy bed!'

Hold all calls—it's time for guests.

LAYER 1 • Paint & architecture With the Murphy bed and built-ins in place, we went for a monochromatic color scheme that emphasized texture over color.

LAYER 2 • Installed flooring We kept the wood floor bare so that our coffee table could roll freely to and from its "garage."

LAYER 3 • Upholstered furniture An upholstered club chair tailored in a silver-gray herringbone pattern adds a touch of refinement. I also consider the sumptuous bed comforter a high-ticket item.

LAYER 4 • Accent fabrics Our drapes and window seat match, so we chose a different fabric for the chic and room-darkening Roman shade.

LAYER 5 • Non-upholstered furniture (workhorses) Three bookcases and a work surface became a stylish yet practical office area. With the money we saved on the work area and rollaway coffee table, we splurged on the Murphy bed and armoire.

LAYER 6 • Accessories Galvanized-metal boxes provide both storage and another accent color, repeated in the mirror and picture frames.

LAYER 7 • Plants & lighting For working, a sleek table lamp and small clamp-on lights; for relaxing, three lights over the Murphy bed and a tin candle lantern.

Guest Bedroom Getaway

Accommodate their yen for Zen

I love being a guest. Nothing makes me happier than an old-fashioned visit to a friend's home, followed by an evening in a comfortable, cozy guest room. I try to return the favor and provide all the comforts of home when friends visit me. If you have a warm and inviting guest bedroom, your guests will feel sheltered, snug, and loath to leave.

BEFORE

This guest room was quite charming, but its layout presented a special challenge. It had multiple windows and doors that snatched up precious wall space. One wall connected two alcoves (one leading to a bathroom, the other to a patio), and between stood a pair of intrusively ugly core doors that enclosed the only closet space in the room. Not only did these doors dominate the space, but they were the focal point from hell!

The closet space had to remain functional, but clearly the art of disguise was much needed. We thought of simply removing the doors and installing a track-and-curtain combo. But the idea of guests opening and closing the curtains every time they needed something drove me nuts. I'd have to be creative and come up with another solution for this dilemma.

TWO BEDS ARE BETTER THAN ONE The idea of two twin beds in a guest room rather than a full or queen bed appeals to me. Two beds accommodate multiple guests and allow them slightly more space and privacy. More important, twin beds have a great look and add symmetry to a room. But where would you position the twin beds in this room?

Multiple windows and doors limited the wall space but not the possibilities in this room. Twin beds were placed in the middle of the room and pushed up to the backs of bookcases, creating a virtual wall. Cornices were constructed from plywood, trimmed with molding, and swathed in fabric.

We thought about placing them under the window, but since the window opens inward it wouldn't be ideal. We considered putting them in an L configuration, but they would meet awkwardly in the center. Blocking the doorways on the other two walls wasn't a good option, either. Oddly enough, it was the closet-door dilemma that became the springboard for the perfect solution to this room ... who knew?

The simple answer was fabric. Fabric would help us conceal those unsightly doors. Rather than replace them, we would create a dramatic fabric scene right in front of them! Yes, two fabulous canopy beds, placed side by side, could be breathtaking in the room, provide a new focal point, and if designed correctly, double the much-needed storage space. Two twin beds smack in the center of the room? Indeed.

You think I'm crazy, don't you? We actually created our own wall right in front of the closet doors, using two inexpensive, assemble-it-yourself bookcases. The bookcases were tall and reached just about from floor to ceiling. To leave enough space to access the closet, we placed the bookcases about three feet from the closet doors. Is that cool or what?

Fabric and color take center stage here. I chose a calming dusty Wedgwood blue for the guest-room walls, and added a bit of cheer with accent fabrics in shades of lemon and butter. Chenille, toile, and formal brocade fabrics add texture and variety.

Molding (Layer 1)
Larger-than-life molding disguises plywood boxes.

Paint (Layer 1)
Soothing blue adorns the walls, with a gray-blue on the ceiling.

Fabric (Layer 4)
Traditional English toile fabric hanging from a cornice lends a canopy effect.

Socket and dowel (Layer 1)
This simple hardware is the backbone of our elegant bed drape.

Plywood attached to the backs of bookcases are our headboards. It took only gorgeous brocade fabric to beautify them. Doesn't the toile fabric look spectacular hanging from the cornices? And it's easy to do!

The twin beds are pushed up to the backs of the two bookcases, which face the closet. We built upholstered headboards in an L shape out of plywood and screwed them into the backs of the bookcases, and for added security bolted the headboards to the floor with metal L brackets. This lower piece fits right beneath the wheels of a regular bed frame. When the guest leans up against the headboard, all the stress goes to the floor rather than up against the bookcases. The bookcases are also bolted to the floor, completely anchoring the unit and making it sturdy and secure. Remember: safety first!

The bookcases line up directly under a pair of breathtaking cornices. Aren't they fabulous? The cornices are simple pine boxes mounted directly to the ceiling

and then trimmed out with crown molding of a substantial size. If this size molding isn't in your budget, just use a little bit of trim molding—it has the same effect. You know me, I like my molding large!

Several of the shelves on each bookcase were left empty for guests to use as storage space. I can't tell you how much I dislike a guest bedroom in which every surface is filled, every nook and cranny jammed. The idea behind this is usually nothing more than an ill-conceived notion that blank spaces are bad. In reality, guests need a little space to call their own. Visitors can wake up in the morning, walk around to their own personal vanity area, and prepare for the day without feeling cramped.

The shelves of the bookcases face the closet, and we furnished them with all the trimmings of comfort—a round mirror, vanity items, and fluffy towels. We also placed blooming plants on the shelves, adding a touch of garden-inspired warmth to the room.

HAVING A BALL WITH TOILE   Inside the cornice boxes, we installed a socket and dowel on both sides for bed drapes that would hang down just like a regular canopy (see pages 138–139 for more detail). I love the color combinations we used for the fabrics. I chose a fabulous blue-and-cream English toile fabric that was shirred onto the entire area behind each bed and cascades from the ceiling down the back of each bookcase. Toile is a traditional repeated-scene pattern that dates back to the 1600s, and it's one of the most popular fabrics used in bedrooms today. We used this same fabric for the side hangings that drape from inside the cornice boxes and tie back to the bookcases, gracefully falling to the floor on either side.

We set the traditional blue-and-cream toile against a very pale lemon-colored fabric that we used for the valance toppers around the cornices. The toppers connect the cornices to the peaks of the bookcases, creating the illusion of a single, grand built-in structure from floor to ceiling. We scalloped the edges of the valances and secured them with Velcro to the pine cornices just below the molding. They add height and scale to the room and reinforce the elegance of custom-built architectural elements. The toppers disguise all the plywood areas of our cornice boxes, and the big fabric drop is wonderfully dramatic.

This room is all about symmetry. Everything is exactly the same on both sides, and the room feels balanced. You wouldn't want to play favorites among your guests, would you?

I chose matching lemon-yellow chenille bedspreads, and pillow shams matching the English toile bed hangings. Even our headboards, upholstered in a formal diamond brocade fabric, are padded and stylish, and complement the toile. The wonderful fabric in this room is functional, too, as it helps to deaden the traffic sounds from a busy intersection outside the window.

Between the twin beds there was just enough room for a small table and a lamp. The table divides the area and helps separate space. We're so used to king and queen beds nowadays. I don't know about you, but I only sleep on about half of my bed. If you haven't seen twin beds in a long time, it's time to say hello again.

Generous fabric panels in a buttery yellow, hung on a simple closet dowel, adorn each side of the double window and look fabulous against the Wedgwood blue wall. We accessorized just one corner of the room, placing two topiaries high on wooden pedestals. Don't forget to keep surfaces clear for your guests!

It's easy to create a beautiful-looking guest room, but usually we don't know if it works well since we don't spend time in it. When planning your guest room, think about the wonderful hotels you've visited. The fluffy bathrobe is always properly placed, and small touches like a basket of munchies for weary travelers and a few complimentary toiletry items truly make a difference in the quality of your stay. Remember: the nicer the guest bedroom, the happier your guests!

OPPOSITE: Eighteen inches of space is all the human form needs to walk comfortably between pieces of furniture. We left walkways clear all the way around the twin beds, providing ample access to the bathroom, patio, and hallway doors. There's no squeeze happening here!

BELOW: Charming ottomans at the foot of each bed provide a clean surface on which a guest can sit comfortably, or place a suitcase and leisurely unpack.

Cornice with class

Like many of our projects, this one starts with plain bookcases. What really makes it spectacular is the cornice box—trimmed with grand molding and fabulous bed hangings. Just be sure that the cornice box is properly anchored to the ceiling by screwing directly into the studs with heavy-duty hardware. You wouldn't want it falling on a guest's head—well, most guests anyway. We made two cornices side by side for our twin beds, but you could make it larger for a double, queen, or even king bed. For demo purposes, I made a smaller version of the box here.

what you'll need . . .

Purchased bookcase(s)

1-inch × 12-inch pine boards

One 4 × 8-foot sheet of ¾-inch plywood (when cut, each lid measured 36 inches × 48 inches)

4-inch crown molding

Closet doweling

6 sockets for closet doweling

Appropriate hardware to secure cornice to ceiling

Saw

Miter box

Screwdriver

Wood screws

Wood glue

Hammer

Finishing nails

Kraft paper

Marker

Fabric for valance and bed drapes

Scissors

Staple gun

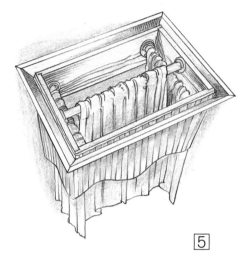

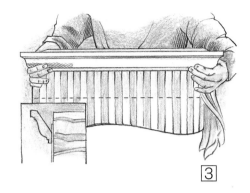

1 For the cornice, use pine boards to construct a box a few inches wider than the bookcase and twice its depth. Make a lid the size of the box plus the width of the molding. Cut the molding, mitering the corners. Attach the lid of the box to the ceiling, being sure to anchor it securely. Screw two pairs of doweling cups on the inside of the box to support the side drapes. Center a third pair of doweling cups side to side for the back drape.

2 To make the valance pattern, wrap a sheet of kraft paper around the box from front to back. Mark the corners, the front center and the back center. Remove the paper and draw a wave pattern along the bottom edge, dipping the wave at the corners and center marks to a depth of 15 inches. Cut out the pattern.

3 Transfer the pattern to your fabric, flipping it over at the center front for symmetry on both sides. Cut out two identical pieces of fabric, lay them face to face and stitch the sides and bottom together. Turn them right side out and wrap the cornice box with the valance, starting at the center back and sandwiching the fabric

between the box and crown molding. Secure the molding with finishing nails. Screw the box to the lid on the ceiling.

4 For the headboard, cut ¾-inch plywood into a house shape. Its height should be halfway from the floor to the bottom of the valance. For support, attach a piece of plywood to the bottom of the headboard at right angles using metal L brackets. The wheels of the bed frame will rest on this piece to help anchor the headboard. Upholster the headboard by laying fabric over quilt batting, and stapling the edge of the fabric to the back of the headboard.

5 For the bed drapes, stitch a hem at the top of three fabric panels. Hang each side drape from closet dowels inside the cornice, and puddle them on the floor. Hang the back drape, twice the width of the bed, from its pole inside the cornice down the back of the bookcase. For further support, anchor the headboard to the bookcase, sandwiching the fabric in between. (See pages 134–135 for more detail.)

Guests need a little space to call their own.

LAYER 1 • Paint & architecture The cornice boxes created architectural interest in this room. We painted the walls a deep dusty blue with lemon trim.

LAYER 2 • Installed flooring We thought of adding large area rugs, but with the paths so narrow, we stuck with hardwood. Guests' suitcases wheel in and out easily, too.

LAYER 3 • Upholstered furniture Like any high-ticket upholstered items, beds and ottomans are kept in neutral colors, emphasizing texture.

LAYER 4 • Accent fabrics The vertical columns of cascading fabric, ceiling to floor, became the focal point the room was crying for.

LAYER 5 • Non-upholstered furniture (workhorses)
Bookcase storage areas are the flip side of the headboards. And where would the alarm clock, water, phone, and lamp go if not for the little workhorse table between the beds?

LAYER 6 • Accessories Accessories were confined to the walls only: a few mirrors, an antique clock, and some reproduction blue-willow pieces. We wanted a clutter-free environment to accommodate guests and their belongings.

LAYER 7 • Plants & lighting Track lights illuminate the center of both beds, and a reading light is close at hand on the nightstand. A view of the garden draws the eye outside and makes the space feel serene and restful.

Child's Play

Anchors aweigh with a cool kid's bedroom

Of all the rooms in a house, a child's room is where you can let loose and have some fun. There are several important concepts to keep in mind, though, when sprucing up a child's bedroom. Although the room should pique your little one's creativity and imagination, it must also be functional and practical. In other words: Where do you store toys? Where do you set up a study area? Where does the bed go? And how do you pull these areas together so that the room doesn't feel disjointed?

BEFORE

I'm a big fan of themes, especially in kids' rooms. When you successfully create a fantasy setting for your kids, it encourages their imagination. In picking a theme, go with what your child likes. In this room, we chose a nautical motif. What child wouldn't want to wake up every morning in this maritime fantasy, with his or her own private ship, dock, and beach? The marine theme transformed this kid's room from just four plain walls into a magical chamber.

To achieve a nautical motif, we treated this room as though it were a theater set. Blue was the predominant color, and to dress our seaworthy stage we created a fabulous three-dimensional backdrop in several shades of blue. This three-dimensional technique is akin to what theatrical artists do with a backdrop on a stage. It's all about the art of illusion, and using a trick here and there to create a fanciful environment.

We took the basic furniture of a kid's room and turned it into fun elements that would help bring our theme to life. There's a boat in the room, but it's also the bed. There's a lighthouse in the room, but it doubles as a bookcase. There's even a dock desk that can be a functional study area, and a treasure chest that stows away toys. Now how cool is that? And trust me, parents—a wonderful themed room will make study time and bedtime much easier for you and your child!

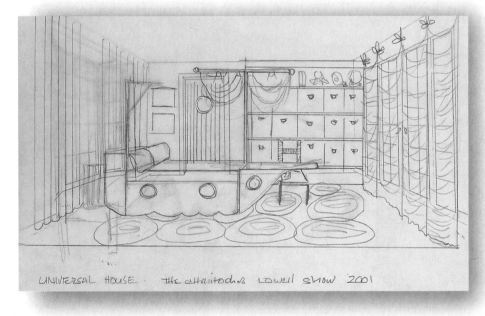

UNIVERSAL HOUSE · The Christopher Lowell Show 2001

Four plain walls will become nautical heaven when I'm finished with this kid's bedroom. The focal point of the room will be a boat bed, easily crafted out of plywood and appointed with marine accessories. We'll add a lighthouse bookshelf and a dock desk, paint a three-dimensional mural, and it's time to set sail!

SET SAIL ON THE S.S. CHRISTOPHER The focal point of this room is a terrific boat bed. The secret is a little plywood and lots of paint. By the time you finish, your child will be embarking on a nightly voyage of discovery, with gentle waves lapping underneath. You'll never have a tough time convincing your first mate that it's time to sail off into dreamland.

We easily transformed a twin bed into a ship using one of our favorite materials, three-quarter-inch plywood. The first step was to make a basic plywood box that would fit around our twin bed. We then added a platform that raised the mattress off the floor. Next, we built our ship's bow and sides. The bow is simply a piece of plywood shaped in a large arch and fastened to the foot of the bed.

To buoy the marine style, fabric and accessories used in nautical life—canvas, cleats, and rope—became our accents. Simple plastic piping was used to create the mast, and toy sailboats reinforce the theme throughout the room.

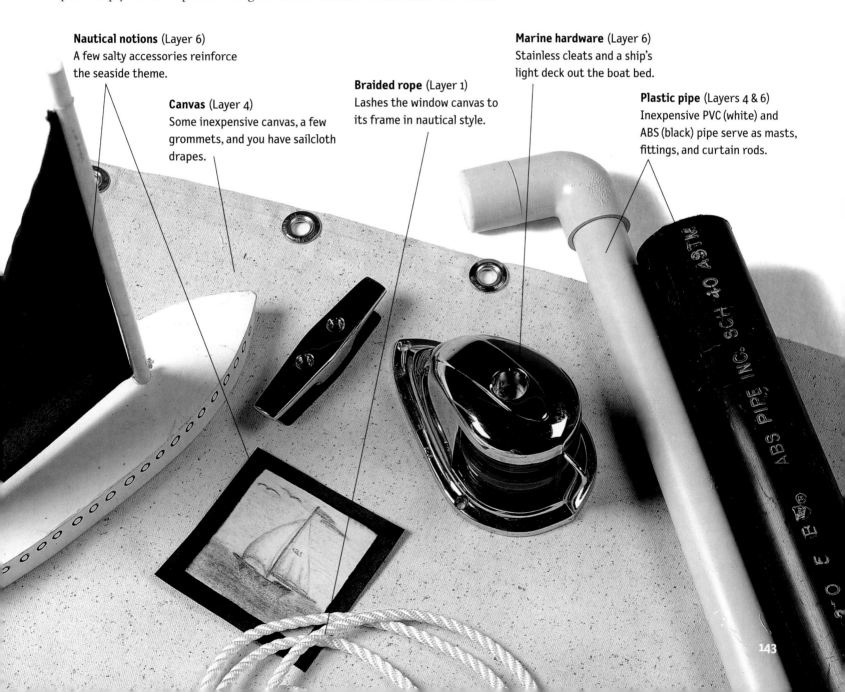

Nautical notions (Layer 6)
A few salty accessories reinforce the seaside theme.

Canvas (Layer 4)
Some inexpensive canvas, a few grommets, and you have sailcloth drapes.

Braided rope (Layer 1)
Lashes the window canvas to its frame in nautical style.

Marine hardware (Layer 6)
Stainless cleats and a ship's light deck out the boat bed.

Plastic pipe (Layers 4 & 6)
Inexpensive PVC (white) and ABS (black) pipe serve as masts, fittings, and curtain rods.

ABOVE: A twin-sized boat bed is constructed from three-quarter-inch plywood, and a raised platform supports the mattress. A plywood arch becomes the bow, while a simple headboard with a shelf and overhang is our ship's cabin. The fantasy bed is completed by adding a mast made from plastic pipe.

OPPOSITE: A whimsical painting technique using overstated, coarse strokes changes the armoire from a store-bought piece into a fantastical cabinet that looks as if it were fashioned from weathered wood.

The next step was to construct our ship's cabin at the front of the bed. Since the slanted sides of the cabin were already formed by our plywood surround, we simply attached a plywood headboard and added a shelf on top, with a slight overhang. Five small circular portholes were cut along the front of the overhang, and we added small lights underneath the shelf. In the evening, the light shines through the portholes and the effect is quite spectacular.

On each side of the cabin, we cut out two large portholes by attaching a plywood disk to each side and taking a hole out of the center of the disk. This left a two-inch raised reveal around the porthole, which added dimension and interest.

To catch the winds, our ship needed a mast which was built out of standard plumbing pipe: a vertical piece of black plastic ABS pipe with a horizontal piece of white plastic PVC pipe crisscrossing it at the top. Next, we used a painting technique that we incorporated into all the painted surfaces in the room (except the boat, which we painted in a nautical motif) to provide continuity of style. It's a whimsical, cartoonish style that makes the surfaces look like wood with very exag-

gerated, grainy strokes. Deepening the illusion, we draped a piece of canvas cloth over the crossarms of the mast to suggest a sail and put a little finial at the top of the mast. How cool is this?

We used the same whimsical painting technique to convert the surface of a plain-looking armoire into a fanciful piece of furniture made from colorful, aged driftwood. An armoire in a kid's room is the perfect place for folded clothes like sweatshirts and jeans, or for books and toys. If your child is neat, you have the option of leaving it open and displaying the contents. But if your kid is not so tidy, just close the doors and it's good-bye mess.

A fun part of building our boat bed was a jaunt to a marine hardware store to buy some maritime accessories for our nautical bed. We picked out cleats and fittings and a ship's light that would also hold our bow flag. Now our ship has a fore and an aft, a starboard and a port. Of course, I can never remember which is which. But nautical terms aside, this is a fantastic spot for a child to drift off and dream.

Our ship couldn't sail very far on any old floor, so we anchored it in a lagoon that we created by modifying the existing floor. We achieved the beachlike effect by laying linoleum the wrong side up over the hardwood floor. Then we handpainted the linoleum, using good old ordinary house paint. Simple, simple! We decided to paint the ocean as it meets the shore, with waves breaking into whitecaps and gently spilling onto the sand. We even added a few little footprints in the sand. You can almost hear the waves lapping at the shore!

'*Kids need a creative, imaginative space of their own!*'

OPPOSITE: A lagoon painted on a linoleum floor becomes a restful anchorage for our boat bed. We carried the scene up one wall and used a one-point-perspective painting technique that adds depth and dimension to our mural.

BELOW: A triangular dock desk with legs resembling pilings completes the lagoon illusion. Once again we employed the exaggerated, fanciful painting technique used elsewhere in the room to add character to the desk and chair.

RIGHT: Decorative pieces like this whale sign bolster the nautical feeling. We fashioned this from scrapwood, then painted and distressed it.

Just use your imagination. This is a great project to do with the kids, too. But wait: we didn't stop at the floor—we continued right onto the wall.

Using a technique called one-point perspective, we painted a sensational nautical mural on one wall. We chose one center point on the wall and drew all of our lines out from that point. To the human eye, the converging lines appear in relative distance or depth. This is a technique I used frequently in the theater when painting scenic backdrops. A little paint can transform a flat surface into a three-dimensional landscape. Now that the floor looks like the high seas, our wall mural looks like a pier and our boat is pulled right up to it.

The mural is serenely nautical with sailboats drifting on the ocean, seagulls flying through the air, and fluffy white clouds floating across the sky. The background is all about illusions. A child can project himself out along the horizon, into one of the boats, or just to the end of the pier.

IT'S A DOCK, IT'S A DESK   To sell this grand illusion, we extended the look of the pier out from the wall by building a triangular-shaped desk from plywood and adding three cut-down posts that resemble pier pilings. The longest side of the triangle is placed up against the wall mural so that it continues in real dimension into the room. The dock is now a desk, providing a wonderful spot to read, work on homework, or daydream about pirates and sunken treasure. Your child has a creative space to call his or her own, and this little bit of inspiration will hopefully open the floodgates of your child's imagination.

The window treatments had to have a marine feeling, too, and we came up with an easy way to achieve it. We made panels out of canvas and added grommets around each panel. We built frames out of PVC pipe, attached them to the door surrounds, and laced the panels into them. This window treatment is cheap, simple, and gives the whole area a very salty look.

TO THE LIGHTHOUSE   The lighthouse bookcase is another focal point in this room. It fits our theme, it's attractive and highly functional. In kids' rooms, storage is essential. Storage spaces should first and foremost serve their purpose well, but it's a bonus when your storage unit has some ingenuity so that kids will want to use it.

We built a four-sided bookcase out of plywood, with a square base and sides that slant inward from bottom to top.

Boat bed

The focal point of the kid's bedroom is this fabulous boat bed. What little salt wouldn't want to curl up in this cozy dinghy, with its bright colors and real marine appointments? This project looks complicated, but the trick is to break it down into several individual components and steps. Most of the key assemblies are simple plywood boxes, secured with wood glue and screws. A table saw and power drill/driver are big helps. As with most of my projects, I first built a miniature version, illustrated on the facing page.

what you'll need . . .

Four 4 x 8-foot sheets of
  ¾-inch plywood

Marine rope

8-foot ABS pipe, 2-inch diameter

3-foot PVC pipe, 1-inch diameter

Canvas fabric

Blue flag fabric

Wood glue

Wood screws

Three "hockey puck" spotlights

Two chrome boat cleats

Marine light

Power saw

Drill

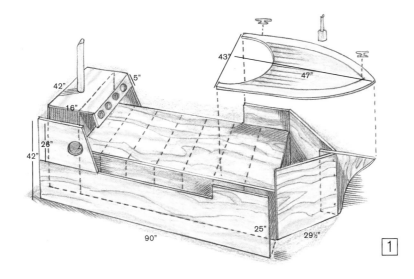

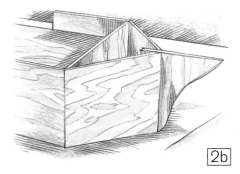

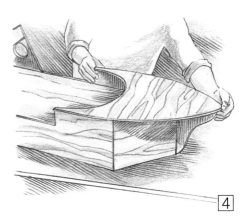

1 Construct a plywood platform for the mattress (for a twin-size mattress: 38 inches wide by 78 inches long by 16 inches high). Install supports underneath the platform, spaced about every 12 inches. Next, build a simple bookcase for the back (stern) of the boat 42 inches high by 42 inches wide by 12 inches deep, with two shelves. Drill 2-inch holes through the top, bottom and shelves for the mast to pass through before assembling the bookcase.

2 Construct two rectangular pieces for the front (bow) of the boat, leaving a ¾-inch space between the two for the prow to be placed. Miter the outer edges of the rectangles to fit flush with the sides and the prow.

3 Construct the two side pieces from plywood according to the illustration. The surrounds connect the bookcase (stern) with the rectangular

pieces (bow) and define the boat shape of the bed. With a jigsaw or coping saw, cut round portholes on each side of the bed near the bookcase. Install a 5-inch piece of plywood across the front edge of the bookcase. Cut four small holes across the front for lighting. Install hockey-puck lights under the top shelf of the bookcase.

4 Cut the bow top from plywood and attach to the platform. Drop ABS pipe through the drilled holes on top of the bookshelf for the mast. Drill a 1-inch hole 6 inches from the top of the ABS pipe and insert a piece of PVC

for the crossarm to the mast. Tie canvas fabric to the PVC pipe to simulate a sail. Cut a flag-shaped piece of blue fabric and attach to the ABS pipe above the sail.

5 Attach chrome boat cleats to the top of the boat bow. Center the marine light near the front of the bow. Make a ladder from marine rope and 1-inch by 4-inch pieces of wood and hang it from one side of the boat platform. Paint the boat in bright, glossy nautical colors, using masking tape for crisp edges.

The angled sides look like the silhouette of a lighthouse. Shelves offer an abundance of storage for books, toys, and games. Even better, this bookcase tower is built on casters and can be moved easily around the room.

You can't very well have a lighthouse without a light! To complete our bookcase, we made a lantern by using closet doweling, overlapped clapboards for the top, and several stacked disks of plywood in graduated sizes for the bottom. The light comes from four candelabra bulbs. We put a little film of translucent plastic around the inside of the light to give it that lighthouse feel. Now this bookcase has all the trimmings of a real lighthouse.

To encourage children to pick up their toys, we decided to build a treasure chest. We took a boxy little chest and place a curved piece of foam on the top. Then we covered the foam with canvas and finished it in the same cartoon-style painting technique that we've used in other places in the room.

We added a little plywood relief here and there with a lock-and-latch combination, and attached a couple of straps. It's delightful to look at, and has ample storage space for all the wonderful little things kids find on their journeys.

Wait, I think the curtain is going to rise on this extraordinary illusion. Our little ship docked at the seashore has its lighthouse, treasure chest, and pier. You could even put stars on the ceiling for celestial navigation. The three-dimensional wall mural pulls it all together. This is what it's all about—giving the gift of fantasy and imagination to your kids.

ABOVE: From bow nightlight and cabin illuminations to a hanging lamp, lighting (Layer Seven) in this room puts the fun in function. The mood at night is like a midnight cruise.

OPPOSITE: A bookcase is essential in a kid's room. This lighthouse bookcase with white paint, slanted sides, and reassuring beacon provides function and focus in our nautical scene. It also swivels on casters to hide the open shelves.

You can almost hear the waves lapping at the bed.

LAYER 1 • Paint & architecture A simple rectangular room is transformed into a gentle seascape with painted murals and trompe l'oeil effects. It looks impressive, but you can do it—really!

LAYER 2 • Installed flooring Rather than use carpet or tile, we created a beach where our boat bed could drop anchor. The waves and dunes flow from the walls onto the wood floor, and for fun we added little touches like starfish and crabs.

LAYER 3 • Upholstered furniture The centerpiece of this room is our captain's bed, complete with authentic nautical fittings and porthole lights. But beneath the paint and trim it's a simple plywood box.

LAYER 4 • Accent fabrics Here we had some fun with authentic marine fabrics, including sailcloth and braided nylon rope. We didn't just hang curtains, we rigged them!

LAYER 5 • Non-upholstered furniture (workhorses) Notice how our "dock" desk continues out to sea as part of the wall mural, and our lighthouse doubles as storage for books and toys. Existing side pieces were simply painted to match the color scheme.

LAYER 6 • Accessories The nautical bits and pieces add a layer of whimsy to the room. Some are authentic boating accessories repurposed as coat hooks or lamps; others were created from wood, rope, and plastic pipe.

LAYER 7 • Plants & lighting The lighthouse beams its friendly beacon … the nightlight glows reassuringly … a swag lamp washes the desk in light. The result is very warm.

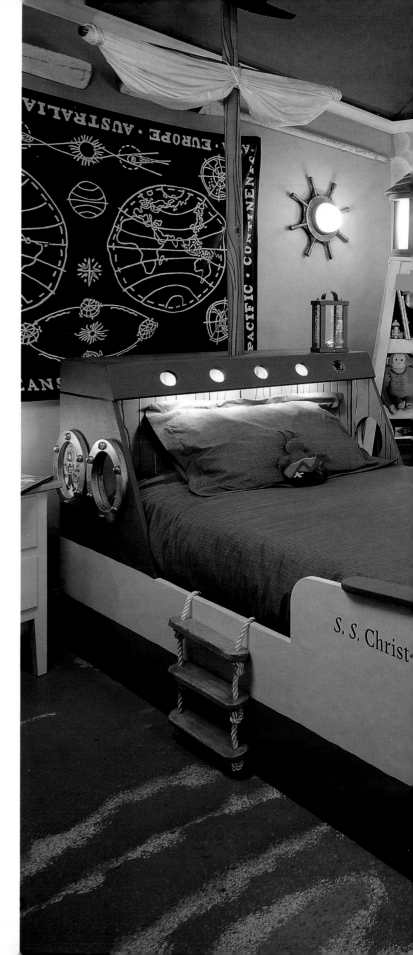

Outdoor Living

A Seven Layer makeover for Mother Nature

BEFORE

Almost every home has an outdoor space, whether it's a grassy backyard, a brick patio, or a small balcony. Spending time outdoors—entertaining friends or savoring little moments alone—improves quality of life. Yet it amazes me how often we ignore outdoor spaces because we think it requires too much maintenance. Outdoor spaces are an extension of your home, so when designing, treat them as you would an indoor room.

This house featured two distinct outdoor areas, the first a walled courtyard and the second a neglected patio off the master bedroom. We tackled the courtyard first, which was highly visible from the living room and the hallway lined with windows. The courtyard would be essential to the house's flow while entertaining, so I decided it should serve two purposes: as a container garden by day, and as a tented dining room by night.

The Seven Layers apply to the outdoors as well as to interior spaces, so the first element we tackled in this courtyard was paint (Layer One). One exterior wall was painted in a deep terra-cotta color, matching the walls of the living room. The courtyard had double French doors, and when they were opened, the indoor and outdoor spaces needed to connect and flow into each other. We achieved this by using the same terra-cotta color both inside and out, visually linking the two together. Now the spaces connect into one casual, comfortable living area—what outdoor living is all about.

We painted the remaining walls a dusty green. Only these two colors were used in the courtyard. The muted green provided the perfect background for the accent colors and beautiful foliage that came in later layers. The earthy colors complement each other and liven up the courtyard without overdoing it. We lucked out with the floor in the courtyard which had terra-cotta tiles in good condition. We saved money here that later we would spend elsewhere.

Yes, my sketch really is of an outside room. Approach your backyard and patio space the same as you would a room inside your house. After paint and new tile for the built-in fireplace, this courtyard was perfect for al fresco frolicking.

FIRE AND WATER   The real focal point and architectural embellishment of this outdoor space is the fireplace. It was in decent condition, but we decided to give it a face-lift by adding some wonderful Malibu tiles, a Spanish reproduction pattern that is frequently found in California. Their terra-cotta and green color scheme was selected with our paint choices in mind. If you can't afford new tile or are uneasy working with it, try stenciling. A great stencil using exterior paint and sealed with an outdoor polyurethane will give you a similar effect without the expense. We painted the upper part of the fireplace the same muted green as the walls, and added candle fixtures above for romantic evening lighting.

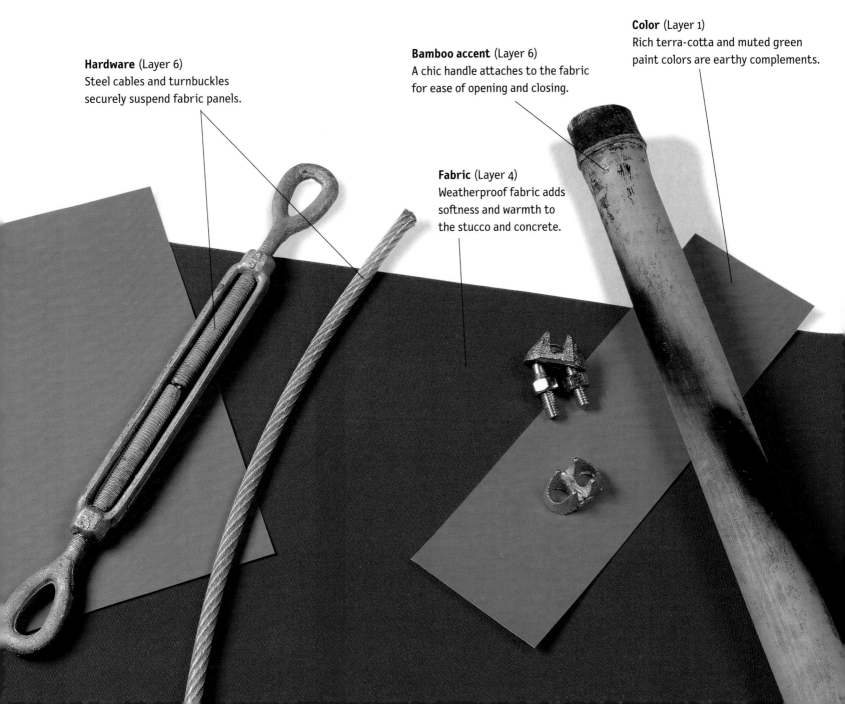

Color (Layer 1)
Rich terra-cotta and muted green paint colors are earthy complements.

Hardware (Layer 6)
Steel cables and turnbuckles securely suspend fabric panels.

Bamboo accent (Layer 6)
A chic handle attaches to the fabric for ease of opening and closing.

Fabric (Layer 4)
Weatherproof fabric adds softness and warmth to the stucco and concrete.

ABOVE: Start with Layer One even out-of-doors. Proper prep work guarantees a crisp finish. Don't shy away from vibrant colors, as light is in abundance outside and will soften daytime hues.

Across the courtyard from the fireplace was a funky but unique fountain that we wanted to accentuate. To achieve this, we cut a groove about ten inches wide around the fountain area, then dyed it a darker color than the rest of the floor, creating a border. We painted the fountain the same terra-cotta color used on the adjacent wall. The fountain had a 1950s look to it, so we just added a new lion's head, making it appear intentionally retro! I love the tranquil and calming properties of flowing water and try to incorporate it outside whenever I can. After being surrounded with plants and lights, the fountain looks and feels stunning.

CANOPY CAN DO   You know how I love fabric. Just because we're talking about outdoor living doesn't mean we have to exclude fabric. There are wonderful fabrics on the market designed especially for the outdoors. Weather resistant, they won't fade in the sun or deteriorate in the rain. What an invention!

In anticipation of our tented dining room, we designed a winch-and-cable kit to string four thick, heavy-duty cables overhead from one side of the patio to the other. These twelve-foot high cables suspend outdoor fabric, the ceiling to our tent. Six fabric panels hang from the bottom two cables, creating movable "walls."

The fabric "walls" are suspended from the cables with little curtain-rod rings. When not in use, the panels are tucked back up against the fireplace. But within five minutes they can be pulled across the suspended cables with large bamboo handles that attach to each panel. Now we have an instant, intimate outdoor dining space. Is this cool or what?

ABOVE: The fireplace was in decent condition, but to jazz it up we added stylish Malibu tiles. Don't despair if tiling isn't in your budget—paint or stencil looks almost as splendid.

LEFT: To make the aging wall fountain look more retro, we literally gave it a face-lift by replacing the lion's head.

ABOVE: The focal point of this courtyard is a wonderful fireplace, perfect for warming up cool evenings. Once the anchors, turnbuckles, and cables were secured, we hung billowing panels of weather-resistant fabric.

OPPOSITE: Who wouldn't want to linger outside and enjoy a meal at this charming table? Open or close the fabric drapes for sunlight or shade, or if it's chilly, light a fire.

A beautiful glass dining table sits beneath the canopy. It's contemporary, but its patina lends a rustic air. We found two wonderful iron grates and put them together as a decorative inset beneath the glass top. You can see the beautiful detail of the wrought iron through it, and there's plenty of space for dinner guests without the dense look of a solid table. We placed a smaller glass buffet table to the side for serving or additional seating. I think using glass out-of-doors is a good option because of its durability, and I love the juxtaposition between the contemporary glass, the antique look of wrought iron, and the formal chairs.

Every good dining room table should have a wonderful chandelier. We suspended a beautiful candle chandelier from the overhead cables. Trust me, nothing beats the flicker of candlelight in the evening. The best part is that we didn't even have to hire an electrician to install expensive wiring.

PATIO PLEASURE   But there was one more patio at the back of the house that was neglected and needed a lift. We evaluated the existing flooring of the patio, which was common concrete, but after years of wear and tear it looked old, dirty, and cracked. We hired a concrete company to spice up the old floor with a special staining technique. Layers of pigment were sprayed right onto the existing concrete. What I love most about pigment staining is its subtlety. This particular technique looks authentic and also withstands the elements. If you hand-paint a concrete floor, in my experience it either doesn't wear well or needs to be repainted frequently to maintain the color. Pigment also collected in the cracks of the cement, creating an antique look. Now the cracks have an old-world look instead of sim-

Look how we transformed a small patio into a delightful meditation corner. An affordable fountain, a few container plants, and two homemade lounge chairs did the trick—impressive together but easily assembled.

ply screaming "I'm broken!" The best part is that we saved a lot of money by modifying what we had and not tearing out the old concrete. Love that!

We inherited a 1940s circular sandpit, the kind that used to be popular for bonfires and outdoor cooking. I thought it looked like a kitty litter box ... no thanks! We replaced the sandpit with a simple three-tiered fountain that happened to be three inches smaller than the pit. To make up the difference, we added potting soil and fern moss, and the fountain looked intentional. How's that for the art of disguise?

I adore the sound of falling water, and it seemed an ideal place for two wooden lounge chairs. If you've ever priced patio furniture, you know that the price tag can give you a heart attack. These reclining chaise lounges (formally known as chaise longues) were made from plain plywood, and the pair resemble outdoor ottomans (see pages 162–163). The cushions were covered with weather-resistant outdoor fabric that we stapled to the back of luan plywood. In inclement weather, just pick up the cushions from the wooden base and away they go into the garage.

This patio seemed the most appropriate place for an outdoor kitchen and barbecue. We added a retractable awning, made from the same weatherproof fabric, to one of the outside walls and created an overhang for the barbecue. The awning's fabric also lent a touch of warmth to the patio. I knew somehow I could squeeze in more fabric!

Plants and lighting (Layer Seven) provided the finishing touches. We flanked the fountain with dramatic orange trees in containers, added two pots of flowering cabbage, then continued adding twosomes of flowering annuals and foliage plants around the fountain for symmetry. We also cleverly flipped birdbaths upside down and used them as pedestals. You know how much I love my pedestals! But birdbaths—who knew?

We included a row of flowering hibiscus in containers against the green hedge in the background. Now we have water and plants enveloping us in this space. All the elements that created this little patio can be hand carried. Plants, pots, and fabric all fit into your car; once assembled and grouped together, though, these elements look substantial and create a beautiful corner.

Most of the lighting for the courtyard and patio is furnished by candles. Shop around and you'll find fabulous candleholders in just about every style, from old world to retro to modern. The soft glow from the fixtures on the fireplace wall, the grand chandelier suspended over the outside dining table, and the small candle groupings sprinkled around the patio enhance the ambience at night.

When decorating out-of-doors, apply each of the Seven Layers as you would inside. From paint to fabric to plants, the outdoor space is your canvas. Use your imagination and create a serene place to spend quiet moments or a hip place to throw a wonderful party—your choice!

'*The Seven Layers apply to outdoor spaces as well as interiors, so treat the out-of-doors as simply another room.*'

161

Chic chaise lounge

The upper-crust call them "*chaise longues,*" but our fabulous matched pair of reclining lounges were made from good old plywood. We were able to replicate the look of custom-built furniture that fits the space perfectly—but without the high cost. The removable cushions were covered with weather-resistant outdoor fabric that we stapled to luan plywood. Hand me my gin and tonic!

To show the key construction details, I built a reduced-size version illustrated on the facing page. The design can be scaled up or down for any ottoman-style piece.

what you'll need . . .

Two 4 by 8-foot sheets of ¾-inch exterior-grade plywood	Outdoor wood putty
Tape measure	Exterior paint
Power saw	Polyurethane finish
Power drill	One 4 by 8-foot sheet of luan plywood
Screwdriver	Three-inch-thick upholstery foam
Wood screws	Water-resistant fabric (3–4 yards)
Wood glue	Staple gun

[1]

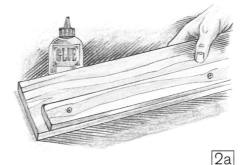

[2a]

[2b]

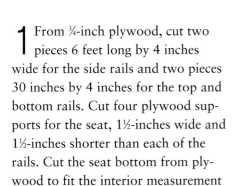

[3a]

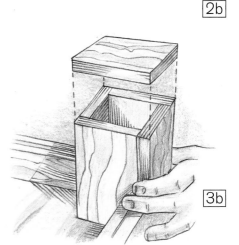

[3b]

1 From ¾-inch plywood, cut two pieces 6 feet long by 4 inches wide for the side rails and two pieces 30 inches by 4 inches for the top and bottom rails. Cut four plywood supports for the seat, 1½-inches wide and 1½-inches shorter than each of the rails. Cut the seat bottom from plywood to fit the interior measurement of the rails.

2 Apply wood glue to the supports and screw them to the inside of the rails, flush with the bottom edges and centered on each rail from side to side. Use a generous number of screws for support. Next, screw the four rails together at the corners to make a large rectangular frame. Place the seat bottom on the supports and secure from all sides, top and bottom with wood screws.

3 Construct the legs from plywood using four pieces for each leg, two 8 inches by 4 inches and two 9½ inches by 4 inches. Cut a 1½ inch notch in one corner of each of the longer pieces to allow for the support (a), position the notches against the supports, then glue and screw the legs together (b). Cut 4-inch squares of plywood for the bottom of each leg. Use long screws from the outside through the rails and deep into the legs.

4 Mix outdoor bonding putty and apply to every plywood seam. Let dry, sand, and paint with exterior paint. For extra protection, coat with a polyurethane finish when the paint has thoroughly dried. Drill holes in the seat to allow for drainage.

5 Make two cushions from 3-inch foam, luan and water-resistant outdoor fabric. Pull the fabric tightly around the foam to the back of the luan, and secure with staples.

Even a tiny balcony can become a fabulous outdoor space!

LAYER 1 • Paint & architecture Bold terra-cotta and deep, dusty green transform the shell of this outdoor space. The fireplace was enhanced by whimsical tiles, and suspended cables with fabric panels create a "tented" room.

LAYER 2 • Installed flooring The courtyard's existing terra-cotta floor still looked good, so we left it alone and splurged on concrete staining for the back patio.

LAYER 3 • Upholstered furniture We built chaise lounges for a fraction of the cost and upholstered them in a terra-cotta-colored weatherproof fabric.

LAYER 4 • Accent fabrics Fabric outdoors? Who knew? I like solids outside, and the same terra-cotta-colored fabric doubles as accent fabric, adorning umbrellas and awnings. It also works well in our tent room as the walls and canopy. How's that for drama?

LAYER 5 • Non-upholstered furniture (workhorses)
Glass and iron are the primary materials in our workhorses. A dining table and chairs provide function, while small side tables are ideal surfaces for resting a beverage.

LAYER 6 • Accessories Large pots and a water fountain on the back patio seem to grow up naturally from the floor.

LAYER 7 • Plants & lighting Orange blossoms scent the courtyard air while trained ivy and hedges break up the wall color. Firelight, candlelight, and even floodlights on a dimmer brighten up our outdoor space when the sun goes down. An outdoor chandelier brings a touch of romance. Remember: what works in, works out!

Resource Guide

Where did Christopher find those fabulous antique beams in the dining room makeover? How do I work with a professional designer? What kinds of tools and gadgets do I really need to work that Christopher magic? Whoa, there . . . it's all here in the Appendix. First, there's a list of sources for the paint, furniture, fabric, lighting, etc., that we've used in the Magnificent Makeover chapters. Then, since I'm often asked for advice about working with an interior designer, I've given you my two cents on pages 170–171. Finally, just for fun, I've emptied my toolkit on pages 172–173. But remember, the most important element of design isn't accessories or gadgets, it's your own unbridled creativity. Have fun!

LIVING LARGE (pages 56–71)

Paint

Wall colors: Clay Cotta, Burned Butter.
Trim color: Vanilla Mist.
For more paint suggestions, check out Christopher Lowell's Color Courage Matching System online at www.christopherlowell.com.

Furniture

Expressions Custom Furniture
401 11th St. NW
Hickory, NC 28603
www.expressionsfurniture.com

Accent fabrics

Stroheim and Romann
718-706-7000
Available through architects and designers.

Pillows

Expressions Custom Furniture
401 11th St. NW
Hickory, NC 28603
www.expressionsfurniture.com

Ikea
800-434-IKEA
www.ikea.com

Tassels

Conso
800-845-2431
www.conso.com
Available at fabric stores.

Curtain hardware

Ikea
800-434-IKEA
www.ikea.com

Decorative hardware

Arte De Mexico
5356 Riverton Ave.
North Hollywood, CA 91601
818-769-5090
www.artedemexico.com or
www.arteshowrooms.com

Candles and sconces

Illuminations
1995 South McDowell Blvd.
Petaluma, CA 94954
800-621-2998
www.illuminations.com

Flowers

Calyx & Corolla
185 Berry St., Ste. 6200
San Francisco, CA 94107
800-800-7788
www.calyxandcorolla.com

Accessories and mirror privately owned.

DINING ROOM DRAMA (pages 72–83)

Paint

Wall color: Braised Cantaloupe.
Trim color: Pasta.
For more paint suggestions, check out Christopher Lowell's Color Courage Matching System online at www.christopherlowell.com.

Antique beams

Conklin's Authentic Antique Barnwood
RR1, Box 70
Susquehanna, PA 18847
570-465-3832
www.conklinsbarnwood.com

Shutters

Allwood Shutters Inc.
1906 Nancita Circle
Placentia, CA 92670
714-996-2500

Leather dining chairs and area rug

Expressions Custom Furniture
401 11th St. NW
Hickory, NC 28603
www.expressionsfurniture.com

Accent fabrics

Stroheim and Romann
718-706-7000
Available through architects and designers.

Tassels
Conso
800-845-2431
www.conso.com
Available at fabric stores.

Decorative hardware
Arte De Mexico
5356 Riverton Ave.
North Hollywood, CA 91601
818-769-5090
www.artedemexico.com or
www.arteshowrooms.com

Van Dyke's Restorers
PO Box 278
Woonsocket, SD 57385
800-558-1234
www.vandykes.com

Curtain hardware
Ikea
800-434-IKEA
www.ikea.com

Chandelier
Arte De Mexico
5356 Riverton Ave.
North Hollywood, CA 91601
818-769-5090
www.artedemexico.com or
www.arteshowrooms.com

Flowers
Calyx & Corolla
185 Berry St., Ste. 6200
San Francisco, CA 94107
800-800-7788
www.calyxandcorolla.com

Mirror and plates privately owned.

EVEN THE KITCHEN SINK (pages 84–97)

Paint
Wall color: Steamed Oatmeal.
Ceiling color: Clam Shell.
Trim color: Pasta.
Shelving color: Broiled Fennel.
For more paint suggestions, check out
Christopher Lowell's Color Courage
Matching System online at
www.christopherlowell.com.

Frosted glass
Bendheim
61 Willett St.
Passaic, NJ 07055
800-835-5304
www.bendheim.com
Available through architects and designers.

Custom wine cabinet
Newkirk and Sons
818-566-1608
newkirkcabs@sbcglobal.net

Stainless steel appliance covers
Frigo Design Inc.
5860 McKinley Rd.
Brewerton, NY 13029
800-836-8746
www.frigodesign.com

Sink fixture
American Standard
800-752-6292
www.americanstandard.com

Cabinet finish
Glenwood Sherry Studios
17919 Clear Lake Dr.
Lutz, FL 33549
www.thatpaintguy.tv
pgshery@earthlink.net

Cabinet pulls, plates, woven storage baskets, and track lighting
Ikea
800-434-IKEA
www.ikea.com

Accent fabrics
Stroheim and Romann
718-706-7000
Available through architects and designers.

Accessories
Ikea
800-434-IKEA
www.ikea.com

Umbra Inc.
1705 Broadway
Buffalo, NY 14212
800-387-5122
www.umbra.com

Lamp
Arte De Mexico
5356 Riverton Ave.
North Hollywood, CA 91601
818-769-5090
www.artedemexico.com or
www.arteshowrooms.com

Table, barstools, and some accessories privately owned.

MASTER BEDROOM (pages 98–109)

Paint
Wall color: Claret and Cream.
Ceiling color: Lowell Lavender.
Trim color: Burned Butter.
For more paint suggestions, check out
Christopher Lowell's Color Courage
Matching System online at www.
christopherlowell.com.

Bamboo trim and bamboo bed
Loose Ends
PO Box 20310
Keizer, OR 97307
503-390-2348
www.looseends.com

Settee
Expressions Custom Furniture
401 11th St. NW
Hickory, NC 28603
www.expressionsfurniture.com

Venetian blinds
Smith + Noble
800-560-0027
www.smithandnoble.com

Caning fabric
Van Dyke's Restorers
PO Box 278
Woonsocket, SD 57385
800-558-1234
www.vandykes.com

Accent fabrics
Stroheim and Romann
718-706-7000
Available through architects and designers.

Faux fur area rugs
Ikea
800-434-IKEA
www.ikea.com

Woven rug and small tray table
Loose Ends
PO Box 20310
Keizer, OR 97307
503-390-2348
www.looseends.com

Hanging lamp pattern
Butterick Co. Inc.
www.mccall.com

Table lamp
Arte De Mexico
5356 Riverton Ave.
North Hollywood, CA 91601
818-769-5090
www.artedemexico.com or
www.arteshowrooms.com

Candles
Illuminations
1995 South McDowell Blvd.
Petaluma, CA 94954
800-621-2998
www.illuminations.com

Armoire privately owned.

BATHROOM RETREAT (pages 110–119)

Paint
Wall color: Claret and Cream.
Ceiling color: Lowell Lavender.
Trim color: Kiss of Grape.
For more paint suggestions, check out
Christopher Lowell's Color Courage
Matching System online at
www.christopherlowell.com.

Tile
B&W Tile Co.
14600 S. Western Ave.
Gardena, CA 90249
310-538-9579

Sink
Aquaware America, Inc.
1 Selleck St.
Norwalk, CT 06855
800-527-4498
www.aquawareamerica.com

Bath, shower, and sink fixtures
Lefroy Brooks
10 Leonard St., Ste. 2 N
New York, NY 10013
212-226-2242
www.lefroybrooks.com
Available through architects and designers.

Faux-finished door
Kurt Cyr Interior Design and Decorations
www.kurtcyr.com

Wooden doorknob
Van Dyke's Restorers
PO Box 278
Woonsocket, SD 57385
800-558-1234
www.vandykes.com

Small table
Umbra Inc.
1705 Broadway
Buffalo, NY 14212
800-387-5122
www.umbra.com

Fabric
Stroheim and Romann
718-706-7000
Available through architects and designers.

Tassels
Conso
800-845-2431
www.conso.com
Available at fabric stores.

Decorative hardware and towels
Ikea
800-434-IKEA
www.ikea.com

Candles
Illuminations
1995 South McDowell Blvd.
Petaluma, CA 94954
800-621-2998
www.illuminations.com

HOME OFFICE HAVEN (pages 120–131)

Paint
Wall color: Walnut Shell.
Ceiling color: Arrow Root.
Trim color: Potato.
For more paint suggestions, check out
Christopher Lowell's Color Courage
Matching System online at
www.christopherlowell.com.

Custom armoire
Newkirk & Sons
818-566-1608
newkirkcabs@sbcglobal.net

Murphy bed
Murphy Bed Products LLC
6370-3 US Highway 1 North
St. Augustine, FL 32095
888-730-3003
www.murphybedsdirect.com

Bookcases, desk, chair, tin containers, desk lamp, and track lighting
Ikea
800-434-IKEA
www.ikea.com

Fabric
Stroheim and Romann
718-706-7000
Available through architects and designers.

Accessories
Ikea
800-434-IKEA
www.ikea.com

Umbra Inc.
1705 Broadway
Buffalo, NY 14212
800-387-5122
www.umbra.com

Mirrors
Umbra Inc.
1705 Broadway
Buffalo, NY 14212
800-387-5122
www.umbra.com

GUEST ROOM GETAWAY (pages 132–141)

Paint
Wall color: Braised Oyster.
Ceiling color: Blue Points.
Trim color: Pasta.
For more paint suggestions, check out
Christopher Lowell's Color Courage
Matching System online at www.
christopherlowell.com.

Ottoman
Expressions Custom Furniture
401 11th St. NW
Hickory, NC 28603
www.expressionsfurniture.com

Fabric
Stroheim and Romann
718-706-7000
Available through architects and designers.

Tassels
Conso
800-845-2431
www.conso.com
Available at fabric stores.

**Bookcases, mirror, lamp, and track
lighting**
Ikea
800-434-IKEA
www.ikea.com

Bathroom accessories
Ikea
800-434-IKEA
www.ikea.com

Umbra Inc.
1705 Broadway
Buffalo, NY 14212
800-387-5122
www.umbra.com

Some accessories and plant stands
privately owned.

CHILD'S PLAY (pages 142–153)

Paint
Wall color: Dusted Mint.
Ceiling color: Kiss of Grape.
Trim color: Cherry Dust.
For more paint suggestions, check out
Christopher Lowell's Color Courage
Matching System online at www.
christopherlowell.com.

**Armoire, trunk, chair, lamp over desk,
and magnet message board**

Ikea
800-434-IKEA
www.ikea.com

OUTDOOR LIVING (pages 154–165)
Paint
Wall color: Broiled Sage, Clay Cotta.
For more paint suggestions, check out
Christopher Lowell's Color Courage
Matching System online at www.
christopherlowell.com.

Fountain and pots
Al's Garden Art
2110 Tyler Ave.
South El Monte, CA 91733
626-448-8880
www.alsgardenart.com

Table and chairs
Christine Vert Ironworks
1437 Lincoln Blvd.
Santa Monica, CA 90404
310-458-6940
vertironworks@aol.com

Outdoor fabric and awning
Sunbrella/Glen Raven
1831 North Park Ave.
Glen Raven, NC 27217
336-227-6211
www.glenraven.com

Umbrella
Hedge Row Decorative Outdoors
1260 Lincoln Ave.
Pasadena, CA 91103
626-398-7990

Plants
Burkard Nurseries Inc.
690 North Orange Grove Blvd.
Pasadena, CA 91103
626-796-4355
www.burkards.com

Chandelier and sconces
Illuminations
1995 South McDowell Blvd.
Petaluma, CA 94954
800-621-2998
www.illuminations.com

Grill
Weber
200 East Daniels Rd.
Palatine, IL 60067
800-446-1071
www.weber.com

Concrete staining
Kemiko Concrete Stain
PO Box 1109
Leonard, TX 75452
903-587-3708
sales@kemiko.com
www.kemiko.com

Paint strips on page 16 courtesy of
Pittsburgh Paints
www.pittsburghpaints.com
800-441-9695

Working with a Designer

Judging from the many letters and e-mails I receive, a lot of you would like to explore working with a professional decorator. Watching the show has given many of you the courage to pick up the phone and call a designer. But finding the perfect match requires a few ground rules on both sides to assure that your experience will be positive.

The designer/client relationship is an intimate one. These are the people who have to know what's in your bedside table. It's their understanding of your lifestyle, with all its idiosyncrasies, that will help them create a working partnership with you. The number-one thing to remember is that you are the boss. You are paying them for the privilege of working with you, not the other way around.

THE FIRST PHONE CALL

Before you pick up the phone, do some homework. Know what you're asking for and roughly what your budget is. What style is your house? When was it built? When was it last decorated, and how many square feet are you looking to redecorate? Let the designer know that you have a few ideas of your own, but are looking for someone to help you implement them. This reinforces the idea of partnership up front.

Ask if there is a fee for the first consultation (there should be). If you decide to move ahead with the job, is this fee waived? I charged a fee simply to make sure that the potential client takes my time seriously. Ask the designer what a consultation will consist of. Tell the designer that although you realize it will be off the cuff, you'd like a first impression. Finally, let the designer know that you will be prepared to write a check upon his/her exit. This lets the designer know that you're up front about money.

I've found that it takes at least three visits with a client before both parties are comfortable about signing off on the project. The first meeting should

be primarily to determine compatibility. The second visit should be financial. The third meeting should be a formal presentation, where the designer shows you specifically what he/she has in mind for your makeover.

THE FIRST VISIT

On the day of your first consultation, have a notepad and pen ready, or even a tape recorder. Rather then waiting for information from your consultant, have a list of specific questions ready: What would you do with this sofa? What colors would you paint this room? Does this floor need refinishing? Don't be afraid to ask. I also think it's important to have both heads of household present when I do my consultation.

Let the designer tour your entire home. It gives he/she an insight into who you are. Don't ever apologize for how you live. If the conversation seems like it's alarmingly "all about them," cut the consultation short. If you detect the slightest hint of condescension now, when they should be on their best behavior, it will only get worse.

At the end of this first visit, you may want to ask, "If we decide to proceed, what will be the next step?" The reply should be something like, "I'd like to come back to the house and have a financial meeting. If we can come to an agreement, I'll take measurements and photos for reference so I can develop preliminary layouts for your completed room."

THE SECOND VISIT

Your second phone call to the designer should be an invitation for a financial discussion. This doesn't mean that you are hiring the designer at this point. It means that you are impressed enough with the designer's creative ideas to discuss the way he/she does business.

The most important thing you can request that the designer bring to the second meeting is an actual profile of another client. This includes samples of the initial design, plus whatever materials he would provide for the clients' approval. This file should also include a series of billings that show how the designer handles the clients' money. A good paper trail means that you'll know, at all times, how your money is being spent. Remember,

anyone can have great ideas, it's the coordination, tracking of funds, and attention to detail that separates the pros from the amateurs.

THE THIRD VISIT

Next comes the designer's rendering. How can the designer possibly communicate what a finished room will look like without a drawing? More important, how will the designer communicate with a multitude of workmen if he/she doesn't have a plan?

As a designer, I will create a full rendering of how I see the room looking when it's finished. If the designer doesn't draw renderings, insist that he/she hire someone to do it. There are professional renderers in just about every city. For a rendering, the client will pay about $1,000. Now this may sound steep, but this fee is refundable if the client chooses to implement the plan. If the client chooses not to go forward with the work, they still keep the rendering. I've had clients who pay for the renderings, then use them as a blueprint to do the work themselves. This is perfectly fine with me.

HERE'S THE DRILL

I make no bones about the fact that I prefer a client who gives me the freedom to put a thousand-year-old vase next to a flea-market bowl. I like to shop anywhere I want, giving the client full disclosure. There's no sneaking around, no inflation of prices, and all sources are known to the client. There may come a time when the homeowner, after the completion of many rooms, will have learned a thing

or two from me and will begin exploring his/her own creativity.

For this reason, I charge an overall percentage of the project cost so I can pass on whatever savings I get along the way. Some decorators mark up each individual item and then take a percentage of the "perceived" value rather then its actual cost. Many will invoice the item on their business letterhead but not furnish the actual receipt. This per-item-markup puts a wall between the designer and his/her client that I find intrusive.

I will charge 25% of the overall project as my fee. Only after the agreed upon project is finished will I charge a daily shopping fee for any little extras. Simple as that.

A third of the money is due once the renderings and the budget are approved. The second third is paid out at the time that all construction, flooring, and built-in fixtures are installed. The final third is awarded when the project is finished.

Now a lot of designers don't like to work this way because the onus is on them to keep track of everything, and have a clear vision from the start of a project rather than making it up as they go. But that's the point. After the vision is created the bulk of the project is getting it done on time and within budget. There, now you know the most important secrets of working with a professional designer!

Christopher's Toolkit

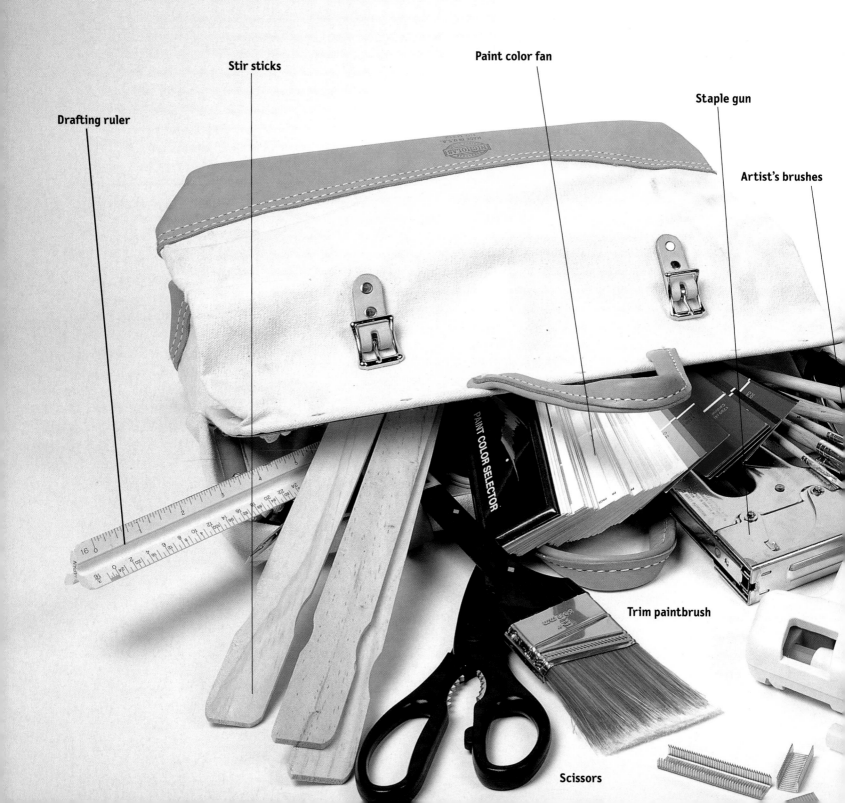

Drafting ruler

Stir sticks

Paint color fan

Staple gun

Artist's brushes

Trim paintbrush

Scissors

I know, it's a bit of a mess. But these are the workhorses of my toolkit, used primarily to measure, plan, and create my room designs before the actual construction begins. There's a tape measure to get the room's overall dimensions, and a ruler to help draft the sketch or rendering. The fan deck of paint colors is my palette; sometimes I'll brush on a small test patch of paint to see how a color will work in actual lighting conditions.

My project demos are usually built from simple plywood or dimension lumber using basic tools: hammer, saw, screwdriver, and drill. If you have no other power tool in your home, a cordless drill would be my recommendation. For working with fabric, you'll need a needle and thread, a staple gun, and a glue gun. These tools also come in handy for small wood projects and repairs.

To this kit I'd also add a flexible filler such as Flexall, wood putty, and sandpaper for finishing various surfaces prior to painting. The cloth tool bag is lighter and less noisy than a big hunkin' metal box.

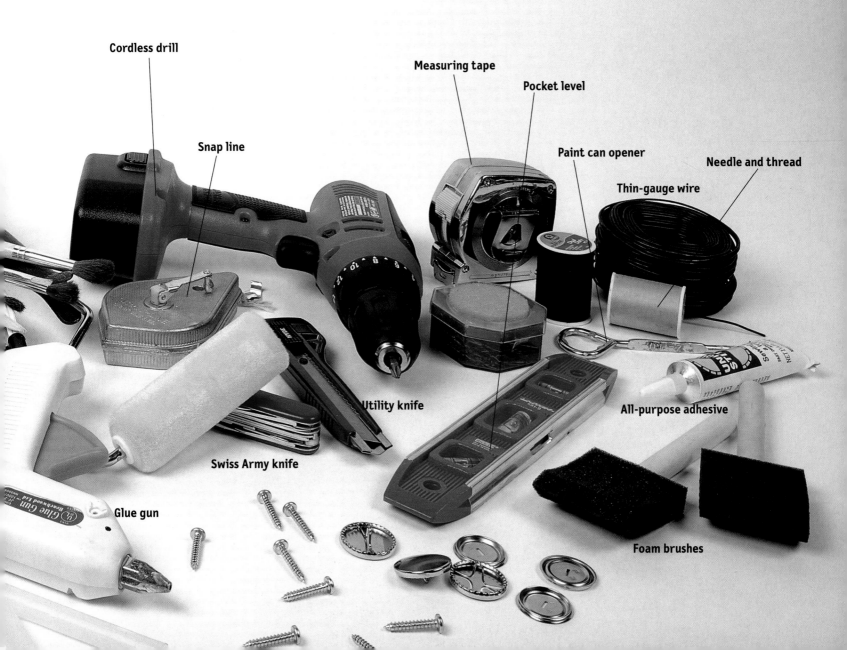

Cordless drill

Snap line

Measuring tape

Pocket level

Paint can opener

Thin-gauge wire

Needle and thread

Utility knife

All-purpose adhesive

Swiss Army knife

Glue gun

Foam brushes

Index

ACKNOWLEDGMENTS

I learned long ago that nothing wonderful happens alone. For that reason, I'm grateful to the following folks without whom this book would not have been possible. First of all, I'd like to thank Michael Murphy who has been in the trenches from the beginning. I'd also like to thank my "Steel Magnolias," the producers (and my friends): Elaine Perkins, Elayne Sawaya, Ele Samson, Dana Neillie, and Terri Davis. Thanks to my friend and colleague, writer Steven Viens. Thank you to the art department, whose amazing dedication to this project under the inspiring vision of Jocelyne Borys helped to make my vision a 3D reality: Jonathan Bowra, Jim Kronwall, Steven Lee Burright, Dylan Berry, Michelle Martin, and Nathan Smith. Thanks to Janet Newell for her tireless dedication to our vision, our viewers, and our readers. Thank you to Susan Maruyama who assembled the best editorial team I've ever worked with: Ken Winchester, Robin Weiss, and Claudia Blaine; with respect and thanks to my photographer and friend, Douglas Hill. Finally, I'd like to thank the Christopher Lowell, Inc., management team at Daniel J. Levin and Associates, and Gerri Leonard and the business management team at Sendyk, Leonard and Company.